"Alexander rightly redefines our under[...] in partnership with God, which God u[...] more like himself. Churches nurtured [...] its gospel-centered principles will beco[...] [...] in places and in ways they never thought possible."

Catherine L. McDowell, Assistant Professor of Old Testament, Gordon-Conwell Theological Seminary, Charlotte

"This is an incredibly important guide. I know of no other book that so fully incorporates the meaning of the gospel and of our work and what it means for my life as a Christ follower in the marketplace. It is equal parts illuminating, practical, inspiring, and encouraging. In the truest sense of the word rich, I am a richer man for having read it. I will recommend it to all that I come across."

Henry R. Kaestner, Managing Principal, Sovereign's Capital; cofounder and chairman, Bandwidth.com

"Following in the footsteps of *The Gospel-Centered Life*, Rob Alexander has written a wonderful small group study on work, which is highly applicable regardless of whether our work happens in the office, on the road, at school, or in our home. Using clear examples, accessible language, and important biblical lessons, Alexander forcefully illustrates the ways that God can use our work to shape us as Christians while also using us to shape our workplace."

Christian B. Miller, Director of the Character Project; professor of philosophy, Wake Forest University

"The Gospel-Centered Life at Work is a fresh take on the challenge to integrate our faith and work. Rob Alexander's dual experience of (1) life in the workplace trenches and (2) life in the pastoral ministries of the church give him a rare capacity to prepare this study. His passion for the Word of God and for the world of work are infectious. What the marketplace needs is not just condemnation and criticism but the kind of life-giving gospel served up in this volume."

David W. Gill, Mockler-Phillips Professor of Workplace Theology & Business Ethics; director, Mockler Center for Faith & Ethics in the Workplace, Gordon-Conwell Theological Seminary; author of *It's About Excellence* and *Doing Right*

"One of the church's great lapses in judgment has been the neglect or disregard of work's importance to spiritual formation. Rob Alexander's experience in business and church leadership gives him a unique ability to address this hole in discipleship and help men and women discover the transforming power of the gospel in their lives and daily work."

Bill Peel, Executive Director, Center for Faith & Work at LeTourneau University; coauthor of *Workplace Grace*

"Rob has done an excellent job of releasing the power of the gospel in our everyday work life. Whether you are a lifelong Christian or new to the faith, this book is a must read. As a business owner, this study guide has reshaped me as an employer, service provider, husband, and father to try to become Christ's ambassador in all that I do."

Dave Marley, CEO, Marley Drug, Inc.

"Too many Christians see their daily work as something separate from their faith, except for their opportunity to share faith. Rob Alexander, in his thoughtful and challenging book *The Gospel-Centered Life at Work,* helps us see that our work is important to God. Even in the tough times at work, God is at work in and through us. This is an important contribution to the life of any Christian."

Al Erisman, Executive in Residence, School of Business and Economics, Seattle Pacific University; co-chair, Theology of Work Project (www. theologyofwork.org)

"God's purpose involves us being at work in this world—a vocation, a calling. Rob Alexander says 'work is one of the primary ways we respond to God in gratitude for all He has done in Christ.' He includes exercises and excellent discussion questions to help Christians in the working world."

Will Metzger, Campus Minister, University of Delaware; author of *Tell the Truth*

"Martin Luther King, Jr. said, 'All labor that uplifts humanity has dignity and importance and should be undertaken with painstaking excellence.' Yet, we often don't think imaginatively enough about how our everyday work serves others. In this helpful guidebook, Rob invites leaders—whether in the home or in the marketplace—to explore a biblical understanding of work that changes both us and the communities of which we are a part."

John Terrill, Director, Center for Integrity in Business, Seattle Pacific University

"Here is a timely and thoughtful study of work as a sacred calling. Rob Alexander has put together a deeply provocative and unfailingly practical guide for the Christian community to think anew about the meaning of discipleship in the workplace. There is so much to ponder in these pages!"

Van Weigel, Professor of Ethics and Economic Development, Eastern University, St. Davids, PA

"Many of the Christians I encounter every day are struggling to find real meaning in their work. Without a gospel lens, work either becomes a necessary evil or an all-consuming idol. Rob provides the gospel lens so desperately needed today. If you want to see your life and work as Jesus sees it, pick up this book and read. You will find it a paradigm-shifting experience that will nourish your soul!"

Jeff Gissing, Director of Discipleship at the First Presbyterian Church of Bethlehem, PA; teaching elder in the Presbyterian Church

THE GOSPEL-CENTERED LIFE AT WORK

Robert W. Alexander

Study Guide with Leader's Notes

New
Growth
Press

newgrowthpress.com

The Gospel-Centered Life at Work: Participant's Guide
New Growth Press, Greensboro, NC 27401
newgrowthpress.com

Typesetting & E-book: Lisa Parnell, lparnell.com
Cover Design: Faceout Books, faceoutstudio.com

ISBN: 978-1-64507-198-3 (Print)
ISBN: 978-1-64507-199-0 (eBook)

Printed in India

29 28 27 26 25 24 23 22   2 3 4 5 6

CONTENTS

INTRODUCTION

We all long to find meaning in our work, to know that our work is valuable to others—and most of all to God. Yet we have all experienced circumstances at work that are hard, painful, and frustrating. Our difficulties show us how much we need God's help for our work to fulfill the good plans he has for this area of our lives.

This study is about the spiritual dynamics of work and life and how God uses our work in the lifelong process of making us more like Christ. This study is a tool to help you build a bridge from your personal faith to your work. It will help you see how Jesus's work for you applies to the work you do every day. (This study builds on themes developed by Bob Thune and Will Walker in *The Gospel-Centered Life* and is meant to follow that study. If you haven't completed that study, you might consider doing so before beginning *The Gospel-Centered Life at Work*.)

God oversees every aspect of our lives, yet at the same time he gives us great freedom in the ways we can respond to our circumstances. The message of the gospel gives us a growing awareness that we are far more sinful than we once thought but at the same time more dearly loved and accepted in Christ than we could ever imagine. Putting our entire trust in Jesus's work for us gives us the courage to be faithful sons and daughters who rely on God's Spirit for the everyday struggles we encounter as we work. Because of Christ's work that cleanses us from sin and unites us to God, his Spirit lives within us to bring us to repentance that restores and reorients us. In other words the Spirit works to make us more like Jesus (to sanctify us) as we work. This process includes two spiritual realities that happen simultaneously.

The Divine Dynamic: God is changing us to make us more like Jesus through our work, and he uses the people around us (coworkers,

1

customers, neighbors, bosses, peers, subordinates, children, etc.) and the challenges of the work itself to do it. The good, the bad, the beautiful (even the ugly) are intended by our heavenly Father for our good and his glory as he restores all things. *The gospel is transforming us through the joys and challenges of daily life.*

The Human Dynamic: At the same time, God is using *us*, his people, as agents of change to sanctify and transform the world. We are the reflection of God's image, his workmanship, and his messengers of reconciliation in our homes, workplaces, and schools. God calls us to love and impact those around us through the work we do, wherever we do it. *God is transforming the neighborhoods of the world with the gospel through us.*

The Bible promises us that the gospel is constantly bearing fruit and growing (Colossians 1:6) in every sphere of our lives—in our home, work, leisure, and relationships. This is true for us as individuals and as communities of believers. Everything we do is being brought into the light of God's glory as God's power indwells and changes us (1 Corinthians 10:31). God invites us to live every part of our lives as worship and to rely on his strength rather than our own (Philippians 4:13).

Allowing our new identity as children of God to transform our work and daily life is a primary way believers participate in God's work in this world. Life's joys and challenges push us as believers toward God, where we ask him to reveal his purposes for us and to guide and empower us as we respond to the circumstances we face. As we ask, God reminds us that we are his beloved children. He encourages us to live by faith as unique reflections of Christ before a watching world. No matter how tarnished our reflection might be, the promises of the gospel encourage us to celebrate who we are in Christ and free us to trust the Spirit's work as he further refines and polishes that reflection.

The way we reflect God's character in our work will take many forms over the course of our lives. We don't need to sit in an office, have a boss, or even receive a paycheck to be at "work." Work from a biblical point of view is whatever activity a believer pursues in the sight of God, for the glory of God, to the benefit of others. As children, we begin our involvement with work by observing others. We become learners. Soon we become students and apprentices entering the world of work. From there we grow in responsibility to take care of our own households, seek a job, or pursue a career. Perhaps we'll move from paid work to volunteering or a second unpaid career. No matter how old we are or what we do, as believers we are meant to see our daily activities as a "calling" or *vocation* given from God to honor and obey him.

To honor God in our work is rarely simple or formulaic. We face many complicated questions about the best way to reflect his presence in our lives. At times we may sense that God is clearly directing every detail of our day and that we are empowered by his Holy Spirit. At other times, our sin and the sin of others seem to complicate every interaction and decision. That's when we are reminded of our need for the power and reality of Jesus to guide our work and our lives.

- *The gospel is for us* when we see people sin against one another, but we don't know how to respond as children who bear God's image and are called to imitate his ways.

- *The gospel is for us* when work is hard and meaningless, because the Spirit gives meaning to our circumstances, enabling us to love and serve selflessly.

- *The gospel is for us* when we don't know how to relate to a coworker, boss, client, or subordinate, because God's Holy Spirit is powerful enough to change us and give us insight into other's needs.

We need to remember that Jesus offers us forgiveness from sin as well as the Spirit's power to understand how the promises of the gospel apply to our particular circumstances.

In this study we'll examine the ways the early church described living by faith, honoring God, and demonstrating our calling as God's people in the work he has given to us. The Bible describes believers as ***Image-Bearers and Imitators, Bond-Servants and Stewards, Ambassadors and Messengers.*** All of these roles have relevance to the work we do. We'll consider these concepts in their first century context to get a fuller sense of how the Bible can encourage us and help us apply our faith to the work we do every day.

1 THE GOSPEL-CENTERED LIFE:
GOD REALIGNS US TO WORK

BIG IDEA

For many of us, work is just a set of things we must do—jobs and activities that can be stressful, unfulfilling, and demanding, and that seem to have little to do with God. For others, work is what defines and gives personal value or significance. But God has something better in mind for his children than either of these options. A gospel-centered understanding of work—which puts Christ and what he has done for us at the center of all we do—transforms work from a set of things we do for survival or validation to become our *vocation*, a calling from Jesus to love, serve, and follow him. This makes work one of the primary ways we respond to God in gratitude for all he has done for us in Christ. It's also a primary way we participate with God's people to bring healing, hope, and gospel witness to a broken world.

A DEEPER UNDERSTANDING OF VOCATION

A friend who just lost his job sits across from you with tears in his eyes. "I know I have a purpose," he says. "I need to know that what I do matters, that I'm doing what God wants me to do."

A young mom shares with her friends at playgroup, "I just wasn't prepared for the drudgery of caring for a baby. I love her so much, but how do you cope with doing the same thing day after day on little or no sleep?"

"My work is so stressful," a hardworking executive confesses. "Even when I'm home I'm connected to work electronically. I know my family wishes I wasn't always 'checking in,' but they don't understand what's expected of me. I don't even have the time to think about God and what he wants. It seems like just one more thing to do."

"I'm trying to get my schoolwork done, but everyone around me is partying," a college student says. "I don't know if I'll get a job when I graduate anyway, so usually I go for the fun. I'm a Christian, but I don't know how that connects to life right now. Maybe I'll work on that later."

"Homeschooling my children was so much work, but I loved it," a mom said. "But now my oldest son doesn't want to go to church or do anything. What was it all for?"

How about you? Most likely you also have questions about the meaning, significance, and motivation for what you do. We all want the work we do to make a difference, yet we feel the gap between the realities of daily work and our lives as Christians.

We wonder:

- Am I doing the right thing?

- What should I do with the rest of my life?

- My work is unpaid; does that mean it's not important?

- Why is work so stressful?

- What if I lose my job? Who will provide for my family?

- Why do I get so afraid when I make a mistake at work?

- Is it possible to go to work and not get involved in gossip and politics?

- Am I a good parent?

- Is what I'm doing making a difference?

These questions are not just about work. They are spiritual questions about faith, meaning, significance, identity, and the struggle with sin. The struggle to bring work and faith together is as old as the fall of humanity. Ever since Adam and Eve sinned, they experienced God's good gifts of work, childbirth, and relationships as broken and hard. We know this isn't the way it's meant to be, but we wonder how (and if) our lives can be made whole again.

In Genesis 1 and 2, we see God at work, creating, separating, filling, examining, and declaring all things good. God's intent was for human life to bind together work, family, personal spirituality, and worship into a seamless tapestry. The need to apply faith to work wasn't necessary before the fall since Adam and Eve enjoyed a perfect relationship with God, each other, and creation. One day in the future, the effects of the fall will come to an end. We will see the end result of Christ's first and second comings. All of life will be made new. Heaven will come to earth and sin, sorrow, suffering, and brokenness will be banished. Life in its fullest sense will be restored through Christ's completed work.

Right now we live "in between." Life is still broken, but something new has happened. God has come to earth to be with his people. Jesus, God-with-us, purchased healing and wholeness for us by his death on the cross. When we come to him in faith and repentance, our sins are forgiven. We are given the gift of eternal life and a whole new life right now.

The power that raised Christ from the dead is now working to remake us and everything we do (Ephesians 1). This is the essence of the gospel message.

Because of these realities, even the simplest tasks we perform by faith become acts of worship reflecting God's character and ways. This is the new *vocation* or calling of those who live by faith. Faith changes everything we do. The sixteenth-century Christian reformer Martin Luther put it this way:

> *When a father goes ahead and washes diapers or performs some other menial task for his child in Christian faith, God, with all his angels and creatures, is smiling, not because that father is washing diapers, but because he is doing so in Christian faith.*[1] *(Author Paraphrase)*

Do you see how living by faith can transform our idea of vocation? By faith we depend on Jesus to walk with us. We rely on his Spirit to guide us so that our relationship with Christ brings life to the wearisome, broken aspects of life. We can participate in God's work wherever he has called us. Whatever our role—student, dishwasher, waitress, stay-at-home mom, working mom, office staff, church staff, small business owner, doctor, plumber, artist, contractor—we do all things with Christ, because of him, and with the Spirit's help (Philippians 4:13).

Christ transforms our work from something we do to fulfill our own goals into something much more significant. All our work becomes kingdom work, done in the service of the King for his good purposes. This gives meaning and significance to the simplest of tasks. Christ called us to live for him; he prepared good works for us to do, and as we respond in faith, we realize that all we do is in his hands (Ephesians 2:8–10). This is what vocation means for those who know Jesus. It's not something relegated to a narrow sector of life. *Everything* is transformed.

The idea of partnering with God through your vocation may not be the way you naturally think about life. For some, life feels like a burden when

---

1. Martin Luther, adapted from "The Estate of Marriage," (1522) in *Luther's Works Volume 45: Christian in Society II.* Walther I Brandt, ed. (Minneapolis: Augsburg Fortress Press, 1962), p. 41.

we don't see that God is sustaining the world and advancing his kingdom through us, his children. For others, work becomes something we hope will provide things we think God can't or won't give us—what the Bible calls our idols. Work then becomes a way to pursue those idols and ultimately pursue meaning and fulfillment apart from Christ. We don't really believe that Christ alone can truly satisfy us. When that happens, work soon becomes a trap where we are either proud of what we have achieved or discouraged by our failures.

Our tendencies will always be to minimize God's presence in our work, making everything a grind for survival, *or* to elevate our own efforts and accomplishments apart from God. In light of this we must see that the believer's work is a partnership with Jesus, who already achieved success on our behalf and offers mercy and grace in every struggle (Hebrews 4:14–16). We need to hold onto gospel truths to live out our vocation in this broken world. These truths include:

- *Daily forgiveness*: We need the forgiveness Jesus purchased for us on the cross for the ways we live for our work instead of God's purposes (1 John 1:9–10).

- *Daily help from the Spirit*: We need the Spirit to change us so that we live for God as partners in his kingdom (Luke 11:13).

- *Daily faith perspective*: We need God to help us see life from his perspective instead of our own (Ephesians 2:8).

- *Resurrection power*: We have to ask for the power that raised Christ from the dead to give us strength and help (Ephesians 1:15–23).

- *God's power and control*: When work goes badly wrong, when we or others fail, we need to remember that God has the final word. All things work for the good of those who love him and are called according to his purposes (Romans 8:28).

Meaningful work is not all there is to life, but a meaningful life is not possible without the knowledge that God is at work, using our everyday efforts for his extraordinary purposes. As we make the gospel the true center of our work, God will use us in his kingdom and use our work struggles to make us more like him.

EXTRAORDINARY PURPOSES IN ORDINARY WORK

This exercise is designed to help you think about your work in a new way—as a partnership with God. God does three amazing things in this world: he makes something out of nothing (creation); he stays in charge of everything he has made (providence); and he restores what's broken (redemption).

As you partner with God in your work, you are also creating, providing, and redeeming. It's easy to miss this, so this exercise will give you a chance to think about how different aspects of your abilities and work reflect your partnership with God. Before you begin, take a moment to think about how your work fits into these three categories of God's work:

- Creative work (work such as designing, development, and artistic endeavors)
- Providing work (production and distribution of services or goods for others' benefit)
- Redemptive work (fixing brokenness, relieving toil, and removing pain)

Note: It's okay if you don't fill in every answer or if you just fill in one of the three aspects. To get you started we've given examples from different jobs and suggested how they might connect to the three aspects. The list isn't exhaustive, but it can help you think of ways that your work is connected to God's work.

EXAMPLES OF CREATIVE ASPECTS

"I enjoy creating products, methods, services or ideas." (e.g., engineer, chemist, teacher, author, student)

"I construct new spaces or organizations." (e.g., contractor, electrician, homeowner, plumber, entrepreneur)

"I like to find ways to connect people who wouldn't normally hang out." (e.g., home group leader, person who loves hospitality)

"I help give birth to people, ideas, or beauty." (e.g., parent, artist, musician, pastor, writer, poet)

"I look for creative ways to talk about Jesus with those around me." (e.g., anyone)

"I envision roles for other people that they themselves don't see yet." (e.g., educator, manager, trainer)

EXAMPLES OF PROVIDING ASPECTS

"I assist people in finding shelter that meets the needs of their household." (e.g., social worker, realtor)

"I help in the harvesting and/or restoring of natural resources." (e.g., farmer, biochemist, engineer)

"I assist in providing the efficient use of a utility." (e.g., utility worker for water, electric, gas)

"I help people govern themselves in a way that promotes flourishing." (e.g., politician, activist)

"I educate people and provide a place for community and learning." (e.g., educator, parent)

"I help others find space (time or place) to pursue rest and leisure." (e.g., artist, musician, park ranger)

EXAMPLES OF REDEMPTIVE ASPECTS

"I help physically, spiritually, or psychologically broken people." (e.g., counselor, social worker, pastor, HR specialist)

"I help to reconcile broken relationships." (e.g., friend, guidance counselor, labor specialist)

"I clean, fix, repair things or people affected by the fall." (e.g., HVAC repair, mechanic, handyman, tailor)

"I troubleshoot to avoid potential problems." (e.g., engineer, network administrator, programmer)

"I fight or prevent criminal activity and promote ethical behavior." (e.g., judge, lawyer, watchman)

"I assist and give hope to people in personal or natural disasters." (e.g., fireman, policeman, military)

In the spaces below, take a few minutes to jot down how your work reflects aspects of God's work.

CREATION

REDEMPTION

A gospel-centered understanding of life transforms work to become vocation— a primary way we respond to God and follow Christ in a broken world.

PROVISION

CREATIVE ASPECTS

1.

2.

3.

PROVIDING ASPECTS

1.

2.

3.

REDEMPTIVE ASPECTS

1.

2.

3.

lesson

TRANSFORMATION: 2
GOD USES WORK
TO CHANGE US

BIG IDEA

Work was created to be a good thing, but after the fall it became one of the main areas where our sin and brokenness show up. However, our workplaces are not beyond God's care and purpose. He is more than able to use the fallen things in life to grow us to be more like Christ. If we keep the truths of the gospel in mind as we pursue our work, it elevates work from a daily grind to the space where God is at work in us to deepen our relationship to him, to one another, and to creation as we partner with him in his plans and purposes.

lesson

ARTICLE

2 THE DAILY GRIND

It would be crazy to think that *all* of the work we do is exciting, fulfilling, or even good for us. Yes, we were made *to* work, but not *for* work; we were made for God. As part of God's good creation, work was intended to bless us and to glorify him. But since the fall, these positive aspects of work are harder to see. Work's fallen nature is easier to relate to. Just as we can look for the three aspects of work's inherent goodness in our daily work (the creative, providential, and redemptive), we also see three fallen aspects. In Genesis 3 we see that our broken relationship with God has brought about "toil" or meaninglessness to our work; our failure in relationships has created a selfish "rule" or bent to all the things we do; and the brokenness and decay of creation has produced "futility" or a fruitlessness to work as we try to be productive.

Consider these work struggles and how they highlight the meaninglessness, selfishness, and futility we experience at work:

- John worked hard at creating a marketing campaign for a new product. The campaign went great until John found out that Kyle (who reports to John) had gone behind John to his boss, claiming credit for the campaign.

- Sarita's coworkers are padding their time sheets. They want her to pad hers too, so it won't look like they are working more hours than she is.

- Susan teaches fifth grade. Henry, a student in her class, doesn't pay attention or complete his homework. Last week, after report cards, Henry's dad called and yelled at her for being a terrible teacher.

- Charles is a plumber. The contractor he is working with is doing shoddy work. Charles doesn't want to lose the job, but he feels badly for the homeowners, who aren't getting quality work.

- June is always bragging about her kids. According to her, they are the smartest, fastest, and most creative kids in the world.

- Sam lays carpet for a living. After forty years his knees are giving way. He doesn't have much saved and doesn't know how he can afford to retire.

- Jessica just realized that she made a major accounting error that will cost her company thousands of dollars. She wonders if she should cover it up.

Each of these issues—competitiveness, betrayal, lack of integrity, covering up mistakes, worries about the future, and the never-ending search for identity and security—are directly related to the way the fall has affected our work. Apart from Jesus and his work in us, work creates a downward spiral where *meaninglessness* in life produces *selfishness* in our hearts, which leads to *fruitlessness* in our work. Solomon's question in Ecclesiastes still rings true: "What has a man from all the toil and striving of heart with which he toils beneath the sun? For all his days are full of sorrow, and his work is a vexation. Even in the night his heart does not rest" (Ecclesiastes 2:22–23).

These are all fuel for the nagging doubts that wake us up in the small hours of the morning. We count on others, only to have them disappoint or betray us. We work hard but are overlooked, or circumstances keep us from getting ahead. We make a costly mistake that affects those we work with. It doesn't matter who you are or what you do—executive, student, missionary, mother, or factory worker—work can feel like a heavy burden. But it doesn't have to be this way. God is a Father who loves his children. He uses all of our struggles, including those at work, to bring us back to him and to make us like him.

Our work was never intended to satisfy us in the ways God can, so when we pursue work apart from him, sooner or later it *will* feel empty. That emptiness is one of God's gifts—a reminder that God alone is big and strong enough to be the source of our comfort, security, success, and acceptance. Our desperation can lead us to reorient our hearts and lives toward the gospel. The truth is that our problems at work have to do with *our* sins as much as the sins of others. Those we work with are not the only ones who struggle with gossip, self-promotion, competitiveness, lack of integrity, boredom, etc. We struggle too.

Think about the examples above. At work we want to be appreciated and treated well. We want things to go smoothly. We want others to think well of us. There is nothing wrong with these things. But what happens when you are betrayed? When you might lose your job if you do the right thing? When others treat you unfairly? What is revealed about what you value most? What is more important to you than your relationship with God? Without the gospel of Jesus, it would be so easy to go along with the broken world…

- for John to gossip about Kyle and try to manipulate his boss too
- for Sarita to cheat along with her coworkers
- for Susan to live in fear of Henry's father
- for Charles to ignore the contractor's shoddy work
- for June to center her life on her children and their successes
- for Sam to fear the future
- for Jessica to try to cover up her mistake

But it is right here, in these struggles, that John, Sarita, Susan, Charles, June, Sam, Jessica, and *you* have the opportunity to see how much you need Jesus. You need his forgiveness. You need his power to return good for evil. You need his Spirit to guide you when you don't know the best way forward. You need him if you are going to bring the light of God's love into your workplace. The Spirit wants to use your struggles at work to remind you of your need for Christ and to drive you to him in repentance and faith.

As we cry out to God in honesty about our fears and frustrations, we become open to what God has for us. The Spirit is able to show us how to walk in repentance and faith. We notice where God is already working. We can be thankful. We turn from the things in our work that we have made more important than God—stuff like people's approval, being right, security, comfort, and identity. We believe in the forgiveness of sins and offer forgiveness to others. We are able to trust God with work's everyday difficulties and ask for his help.

We don't have to be stuck in our sins or in those committed against us. We can relate to God differently because of what Jesus has done and come to God as beloved sons and daughters. The gospel that is redeeming and transforming our hearts is the same gospel at work to renew and heal the world.

In Romans 8:20–30 Paul says that God is allowing all of creation (not just you and me) to be frustrated by sin. We all feel the toil and pain that come from it. God does this so that our needy state would push us toward Christ, so that we would know the freedom he gives us as children of God. At the point of our deep weakness—in our futility and despair— the Spirit can help us cry out for aid from our heavenly Abba Father to intervene in things beyond our control. With "groaning too deep for words," even in hard circumstances, God is working things together for our good and his glory.

A life of ease is not necessarily an indicator of God's presence. The Bible says that the opposite can be true as well—that trials and trouble can also indicate God's faithful presence and deep love for us (2 Timothy 2:10–12). First Peter 1:7 says that while it is okay to grieve over various trials, we should also rejoice because trials test the genuineness of our faith and refine us while bringing praise, glory, and honor to Christ.

We can and should be frustrated, disappointed, and even angered by the ways sin has broken everything (the loss of a job for a righteous decision, broken relationships, credit for your good work going to someone else, financial rewards that don't materialize, posturing and posing by others, etc.). But it is not okay to accept things as they are. The Spirit stands ready to do more than we can do in our own strength. We must make room for him and in repentance and faith hold to God's promises to us. Because Jesus is with us, work is no longer a burden we bear alone. Instead, it is shared by Jesus, an opportunity to experience God's love more deeply and to be transformed in and through the struggles, challenges, and disappointment of work. All this happens in the power of the Spirit and in light of the truth of the gospel.

2

HOW WORK REVEALS OUR HEARTS

Let's begin identifying the ways we look to something other than Jesus to provide us with satisfaction in life. Because work so often touches our deepest needs for significance, success, and security for ourselves and our families, it is a prime place to see where our hearts are drawn to something other than Jesus and his purposes. Whether we spend our days as a student, executive, stay-at-home parent, or caregiver for an aging parent, we all struggle with keeping the gospel at the center of what we do. The toilsome and painful parts of work always cause us to ask, "Is Jesus enough to truly satisfy me?" or "Am I relying on my work to provide me with something I think Jesus either cannot or will not give me?"

Take a look at the chart below. It describes the way our deeper heart motivations are revealed by the importance we put on external things.

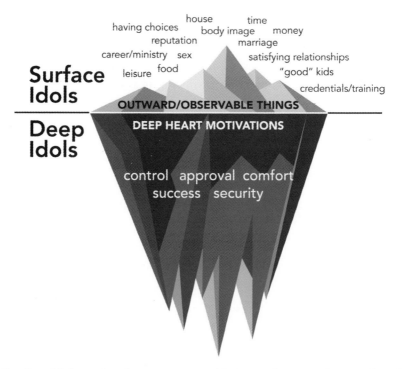

Surface idols tend to be concrete, specific items that are often good and basic things in our life and work. When they come under the control of our deeper idols, however, they go from being good things to ultimate things—things we think we simply must have, often at any cost. As good and basic things, most of the time they continue to remain in our work and life, but they need to be "put in their place" by applying the gospel to detach them from deep idols and put them under the guidance of the Spirit.

Deep idols are the subtle, basic motivations for work that exist at the level of personal drives and character traits nurtured over a lifetime. Because they are so deeply embedded, they tend to express themselves indirectly through good and basic things, turning them into ultimate motivations. Often a single deep idol can manifest itself in a number of different outward actions and attitudes. Applying the gospel to these deep idols helps us repent of seeking what they offer apart from God.

As you look at the chart, discuss the following questions:

1. In your work life, where do you tend to struggle with "good and basic" things becoming "ultimate" things? (List below a few of the "good and basic" things that are operating as surface motivations.)

(a)

(b)

(c)

2. What do you *really* want from these "good and basic" things? What deeper fears, idols, or desires might subtly underlie your list of surface idols to make the "good and basic" things "ultimate" things in your work?

(a)

(b)

(c)

3. When it comes to your work, how would you complete the following phrase based on your answers to the two previous questions:

    Jesus + _____ = *my happiness*

4. Start the repentance process by writing out a prayer, telling God what is most important to you and why. Ask him to forgive you for not trusting in his love and care. Ask him for his Spirit to help you put him first in your life and to remind you when you try to find life apart from him.

3 FROM TOIL TO FAITH:
DESIRING A NEW WAY TO LIVE

BIG IDEA

This lesson helps us identify patterns in the ways we fail to integrate our faith with our work. These patterns often point to the deep idols that undermine the way we relate to our heavenly Father and our neighbors as well. First, we'll see how our "functional idols" might be affecting our behavior; then we'll consider the ways we need to repent and welcome the work of the Holy Spirit in our lives (2 Corinthians 5:17).

Our status as God's children compels us to put off sin and to put on a new way of living by faith—to shed old ways of relating and to welcome new gospel-centered ones instead (Ephesians 4 and Colossians 3). A gospel-centered understanding of work leads us to repent of "bent" coping patterns and deep idols and to more fully participate in God's work in the world as we are conformed to the likeness of Jesus.

OUR FLAWED METHODS

In the Bible, God often called his people to live in the midst of pluralistic societies—Egypt, Canaan, Babylon, and the Roman Empire.[2] As post-modern people, we live in similar circumstances. Even though Western culture was built on biblical values, our society is now almost completely pluralistic and often antagonistic to the gospel. How should we live in such a society and how can we engage those around us where we study, live, work, and play?

- Your supervisor says "Copy these articles and get them to the client by the end of the week!" You both know that the articles were copyrighted by a direct competitor. To copy them would be wrong (they aren't your company's intellectual property), but to quit your job over a foolish demand feels wrong too. You've invested years of your life in this place to try and make a difference—and you need the income.

- Class rank will affect your opportunities for internships and graduate school recommendations. Your closest competitor for the top five percent of the class cuts corners in his research but has escaped detection. He's less careful about racist and sexist remarks, which you know would affect his grades if your professor knew about them. Do you bring them to your professor's attention? After all, you aren't lying.

- A group of stay-at-home moms begins discussing a new family in the neighborhood who are from another culture. They make some stereotypical jokes about the family and wonder why you don't join in.

---

2. A pluralistic society is a culture or environment that expects its citizens or members to accept a broad set of often contradictory personal beliefs in others.

What should we do when we're asked to participate in something morally wrong? Christians have responded in three ways to such dilemmas.

Pretending. The first response GIVES IN to expectations and demands that are sinful, immoral, unwise, or unlawful, either because of an uncritical acceptance of workplace values or an indifference to doing wrong. Sometimes this response is rationalized by distorting the gospel truth that we're forgiven for the sinful things we do. The response may reflect a failure to connect personal faith to public life. For these reasons, this approach has been called "license" or "pretense" because we're pretending (or being fooled into thinking) that what we're doing doesn't matter—we'll be forgiven anyway. We fool ourselves into thinking that we aren't sinning or grieving God if our intentions are good or if someone is forcing us to do what is wrong. But neither case allows us to sidestep the commands of Scripture and be forgiven or excused.

Performing. The second set of responses centers around NOT GIVING IN to unbiblical values or demands. And while it is a good thing to uphold the commands of Scripture, sometimes it leads people to remove themselves from the problem as if it were THE test of their personal righteousness. We call this a "performance" or self-righteous approach because we wind up trying to prove our own righteousness instead of relying on Christ's.

For example, in the case of the copyright violation, a person with this mindset would see quitting his job in protest as the *only* legitimate choice. But that leaves the situation unchanged. A new employee might be asked to do the same thing and the patterns and structure of sin in that workplace will continue. If we remove ourselves from the situation to demonstrate our own righteousness, we lose the opportunity to come alongside our coworkers to help solve the problem and positively impact the work culture.

We need to remember that our right beliefs are never the source of our goodness, and the main problem for non-Christians is not their value system, but the fact that they don't know Christ. If neither of these previous two responses is appropriate, how should we work differently as Christians?

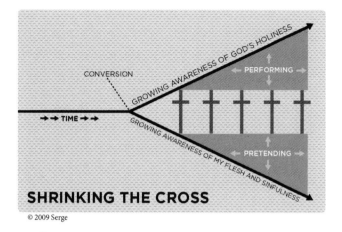

SHRINKING THE CROSS

© 2009 Serge

A gospel-centered perspective: in, not of, the world. A third response to the problem asks, "How can I, as a child of God, uphold God's commands *and* meet the true needs of my workplace?" Answering that question helps us uphold biblical commands while respecting the legitimate needs of those in authority.

To understand this third way, we need to see the ways that pretense and performance are similar. Both assume we've been abandoned in our circumstances and that the gospel is powerless in our situation. We thus feel compelled to rely on ourselves. We adopt an orphan mind-set, where we believe that we are alone and without resources. Instead of trusting God to give us the strength and wisdom to do what is right as his children, we turn to pretending and performing.

When the promises and power of the gospel shape our lives, we grow in our awareness of two things: (1) our awareness of God's character grows—his love, holiness, power, and presence—in ways that make us rely more on him and less on ourselves; (2) our sense of our own sinfulness grows. We see more how the fall has touched every action and thought—even motivations we thought were pure now seem affected by sin. This is not merely head knowledge but something we experience.

God doesn't want us stuck in performance or pretense. He wants us to be people who can repent of our sins, admit our weaknesses, and work, pray, and act in reliance on him. He wants us to seek the prosperity and peace of others. As his people, God wants us to be "set apart" in the way we live for him. At the same time, he wants us to be "set among" those around us so that we do not isolate ourselves from a common life with those who do not know him (Jeremiah 29:5–6).

A gospel response to pretense and performance requires us to rely on God's promises, power, and love more deeply, since we understand that our sinful nature affects everything we do. Without a gospel perspective, we are vulnerable to the pressures of our work culture, whether as a student we are tempted to undermine a competitor or as a stay-at-home mom we are tempted to gossip or as an employee we are tempted to do something illegal because we (probably) won't get caught and we don't want to upset our supervisor.

What if, in the case of the demanding supervisor, the office-worker was willing to work overtime to rewrite the required article from scratch to make the deadline rather than copy the specifications and pass them off as his company's work?

What if the student chose to trust God for his future and rather than use his rival's comments to undermine him, talked with him directly about how damaging his comments were?

What if the stay-at-home mom had compassion on the family being gossiped about, reaching out to them and encouraging friends to do the same?

A gospel-centered perspective is a powerful alternative to the temptations and motivations associated with "pretend" and "perform." When we perform, we rely on ourselves to look better than others; when we pretend, we give in to temptation, thinking (falsely) that we have no choice. A reliance on Jesus's power and righteousness gives us what we need to navigate these dangers in a way that honors God and loves others. In every tension, God is working through us to change our work cultures for his glory while he is transforming us by the gospel.

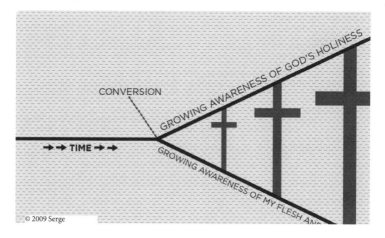

© 2009 Serge

Becoming more aware of our own sins and failures is no fun! It means admitting that we aren't as good as we make ourselves out to be. We need to rest in Jesus's righteousness if we are to face our own sinfulness honestly. Otherwise, our guilt, shame, and regret will turn us back to our functional idols, like making money, achieving success, and looking good, even when we know deep inside that we've failed in many ways.

Growing in our understanding of God's holiness isn't easy either. It means relying on him rather than ourselves. It means facing his displeasure over our sins and repenting for them. If we aren't resting in what Jesus has done for us, we'll end up working harder in the same old ways, trying to earn God's favor rather than relying more deeply on his grace.

In the next seven lessons we'll look at seven ways to turn from performance or pretense toward a gospel-centered perspective in our work. The gospel deepens our reliance on Christ and the power of the Spirit. We will see our need for Christ more clearly and allow God to increase the impact of the cross in our lives.

This side of heaven we will always find ourselves in need of repentance, and the repentance the Spirit works in us will lead us to rest more deeply in Christ's perfect obedience to obey him more willingly and joyfully. Christ lived the perfect life for us, so we can be led by his Spirit to advance his kingdom in this world.

EXERCISE

3 PRETENDING AND PERFORMING AT WORK

At home, work, or school, we can be controlled by pretense- or performance-oriented motivations rather than a gospel-centered perspective. Sometimes the problem is our environment itself and the assumptions and expectations operating there. Sometimes the problem lies in the attitudes we bring to our work. How does it happen with you?

1. Think of a situation at work where you have been struggling.

2. Use the questions below to understand the way this situation tempts you to pretend or perform—or perhaps both at different times.

   (a) Are you tempted to give in to immoral, unethical, or unwise demands placed on you?

   (b) Do you think you have to give in because it will affect your future if you don't?

   (c) Do you excuse your behavior because it's the fault of the person who asked you to do it and God will forgive you anyway?

   (d) Do you overlook others' wrong behavior because you fear retaliation?

   (e) Do you think it's not your problem if you aren't directly involved?

(f) Do you distance yourself from workmates when you don't want to be associated with their actions?

(g) Do you decide not to confront a wrong because you don't think anyone will listen?

3. What desires and fears might be motivating your choices? Circle the statements in the first and last columns of the Gospel-Centered Response chart that apply to the way you are thinking and responding to your struggle at work.

4. Use the center column of the Gospel-Centered Response chart below to answer this question: How does the gospel *call* me, *free* me, and *empower* me to respond differently to this situation?

5. Share what you have learned with the rest of the group, and pray for each other.

Pretense-Based Response	Gospel-Centered Response	Performance-Based Response
Obedience doesn't matter; I'm accepted.	I'm accepted, therefore I obey.	I obey, therefore I'm accepted.
My motivations are pragmatic—base on the values of my work context alone.	My motivation is based on gratitude and joy for being called to where I'm placed.	My motivation is not to do the wrong thing because of the potential consequences.
God has left me to my own devices and abilities—faith doesn't relate to this matter or my work.	I respond to God in delight and gratitude because he calls me his own and I resemble and reflect him.	I respond to God in order to get things from him. He's only generous when I obey.
When circumstances go badly, I am angry at myself since I believe that my decisions should lead to a comfortable life.	When circumstances are unfavorable, I remind myself that my punishment fell on Jesus and that God allows all the circumstances in my life so that I'll be more conformed to his character.	When circumstances go wrong, I am angry at God since I believe that anyone who makes good decisions deserves a good life.
When others critique me, I am devastated because I am so identified with my decisions and work. Any negative evaluation of my work comes at great personal cost because work is my identity.	When criticized, I may struggle, but it is not critical for me to think of myself as a "good person." My identity is not built on my record or my work alone, but on God's love for me in the person of Christ.	If I face criticism, I am furious because I think of myself as a "good person" and my positions are always well thought through. Criticism threatens my value system and even the will of God.
The main purpose of my prayer life is to help me better control my environment. Prayer only changes my heart.	My prayer life consists of generous stretches of praise and adoration. My main purpose is fellowship with God.	My prayers consist largely of petitions for circumstances and heat up when I am in a time of need or feel pressures in life.
My identity is based mainly on how hard or smart or craftily I work and so I look down on those I perceive as lazy, unintelligent, or unwise. I both disdain and feel superior to those around me.	My self-view is not based on personal achievement. In Christ, I'm sinful and also a beloved heir. I'm so bad off that only Jesus could die for me and so loved me he gladly died in my place. As someone who is saved by grace, I don't perceive others as too different from me.	My self-view centers upon my living up to my own standards or goals. When I do, I feel confident. If I don't, I feel inadequate. This makes me prone to a lack of mercy or patience toward failing people.

REVIEW AND INTRODUCTION TO LESSONS 4-9

In the past three lessons, we've seen that our work is one of the major contexts through which we reflect God's character and glory to the world. We've looked at how our work changes the world, how we are changed by God through our work, and how we often get our perspective on faith and work wrong.

We now want to look at how, as believers, we can bring a gospel-centeredness to our work as we move in partnership with God. We want to examine ourselves as

1. partners in God's creative work as Image-Bearers and Imitators;

2. partners in God's providence as Bond-Servants and Stewards; and

3. partners in God's redemptive work as Ambassadors and Messengers of the gospel.

Our last lesson looks at how God partners with us and renews us in our Sabbath from work.

In the next six lessons, we'll look more deeply into each of these six aspects of our partnership with God, using the gospel as our lens and our guide.

CREATION

Image-Bearer
The gospel transfoms my perspective on work from being an idolatrous temptation or source of toil, pain, and frustration to become a way to reflect God's image in my daily life.

Imitator
The gospel changes my work from something done for personal gain to something I do as an imitator of God who welcomes carrying out his will.

Messenger
Rather than being consumed with my own agenda, the gospel changes my perspective to see that life is full of opportunities to engage those who don't know Christ with the seeds of the gospel.

REDEMPTION

Bond-Servant
Rather than my work becoming my identity, the gospel offers me true personhood as a trusted member of God's family.

Ambassador
When I view everyday life and work through gospel lenses, instead of seeing others with competition or judgment, I see my neighbors as God sees them—broken people who need Jesus just as much as I do.

Steward
God's provision for me as his child transforms my orphan attitudes about resources like time and money to uncover ways to seek the good of others with everything he has entrusted to me.

PROVISION

Letting the gospel speak into daily life is a primary way believers participate in God's work of creation, providence, and redemption in the world.

4

IMAGE-BEARERS:
A GOSPEL LOOK AT THE IMAGE OF GOD

BIG IDEA

When our eyes are opened to God's work, we participate in it just by seeing the world from a gospel perspective—being observant wherever he has placed us, ready to speak and act according to what we've come to know through faith in Jesus. Our adoption into God's household as well-loved children qualifies us to walk in partnership with him. Our work—though we are tugged in so many different directions by people and institutions that want to conform us into *their* image—is nevertheless being transformed by God through our faithful gospel presence. It is no accident that God has placed you where you are. Through your presence, you reflect God's character as one of his *Image-Bearers* to those around you.

lesson

4 IMAGE-BEARERS IN GOD'S ECONOMY

The English word *economy* comes from a Greek word that means the "good housekeeping" or stewardship of something or someone. The picture that the Bible paints of God's economy, or work in human history, is one of God's deep love and care for humanity, coupled with an invitation to participate in the ongoing growth, redemption, and care of his kingdom. We enter into God's economy or household when we receive the gospel by faith. God then invites us to become image-bearers who imitate his care for his creation as partners in his household work.

As participants in the institutions of the world that are ordained by God but also fallen (media, government, education, entertainment, households, businesses, science, etc.), we may have once operated without a knowledge of the gospel. Without Jesus, we relied on our own devices and were pressured by those same institutions to be conformed to their "image." Each one has its own language, values, and rewards apart from (and sometimes opposed to) the purposes of God. Even now, those institutions are at odds among themselves as they seek to make all human culture subservient to their goals, aims, and values.

But the gospel has changed all that for us. Jesus, the firstborn of creation, became human to show us how to be *truly* human. He bore the truest image of both man and God for us to see. Through the victory of his life, death, and resurrection, Jesus reversed the curse of sin and death present in us and the institutions we are part of. He gives believers his life and record and makes us partners in his work. Just as the eyes of Elisha's servant were opened to God's work and thus to new ways of relating to his enemies, so God uses the gospel to open our eyes to new ways of relating to believers and unbelievers in our work.

Ephesians 4 says that because Jesus made us recipients of God's grace (Christ's righteous record) he also gave us other gracious gifts—like joy, peace, patience, and kindness—that reflect God's image and character. Not only do we have a tremendous calling and freedom in our work, we also have all the resources we need from God to accomplish the tasks set before us. The grace of God is unleashed by faith and empowered by the Spirit to build up God's kingdom through our work.

Let's consider some aspects of image-bearing in our work.

Our work has eternal purposes. As human beings we've always borne God's image, but now, because of Christ's transforming work in us, the image we reflect resembles him more clearly. We are less likely to use God's gifts selfishly, either to win his favor or for personal gain. Now a central part of our calling is to just be present *as* image-bearers who are ready to respond to what God is doing. Jesus promises to be present with us and to work through us, so our task is to show up, pay attention to what he is doing, and apply his power and perspective to the work before us.

This principle is illustrated in the story of three stoneworkers who were building a cathedral. A stranger wandered by as the first stoneworker was transferring rocks to a pile near a wall. "What are you doing?" asked the stranger. "Can't you see that I'm carrying rocks?" he replied. The stranger asked the second worker, "What are you doing?" He said, "I'm building a wall." Later, the man came upon the third mason. "What are you doing?" he asked. This worker knew whose image he reflected. "I'm building a cathedral to the glory of God!" A godly perspective on his circumstances made all the difference.

Our work points to Jesus's work. Not only do we bear God's image, but because our work flows from what Jesus has done for us, we do our best at work to honor him. We don't have to earn our righteousness or our relationship with God—that comes from Jesus. But now, as God's children, we desire to bring glory to the family name, just as Jesus did. Not only do we want to do good work, we want to work with humility. Now our goal is giving away glory rather than hoarding it for ourselves.

Our work is empowered by the Spirit. Believers are promised God's indwelling power through his Spirit. We will be called into situations where we are incapable in our own strength of doing the work at hand. But Scripture says that these are the times when God displays his miraculous power in ways that others will recognize are not from us, but from him. We will have trials. Sometimes we will be put in harm's way and restored; sometimes we will be under pressure right up to our breaking point. In it all, God awaits our prayers for his kingdom to come and his will to be done on earth as it is in heaven.

Our image-bearing points to the true Image-Bearer. Many people who don't know Jesus do excellent work. Their motivations might be mixed, but we can praise them for it, thankful for the common grace God extends to all his creatures for his honor and their benefit. God puts us in situations where we need to work with unbelievers and share our gifts. There we can share the reason for the hope we have, as Jesus has met us in our place of need and given us new hope and perspective for our lives and our work.

This past year God placed a new friend in my life through some extraordinary circumstances. The "extraordinary" story is ordinary in the sense that God used everyday people in their daily callings to point someone to himself. My new friend had a successful business, a loving family, and outwardly seemed to be thriving. But inwardly he was disappointed; somehow life had fallen short of his expectations. One evening while playing hockey, he fell to the ice and was whisked away to the hospital with a brain aneurysm. He underwent surgery and in those moments cried out to God to spare him. God answered his prayers.

Believers who were doctors, moms, students, and friends surrounded, prayed for, and cared for this man and his family—just as Jesus asks us to love our neighbor as ourselves. These believers pointed the family to what God had done and was doing. My friend left the hospital a different man, humbled by God, eager to learn more about Jesus, who he saw in those who cared for him and his family.

The Good Samaritan is a model neighbor. As he went about his normal tasks, he encountered someone with a desperate need. He responded faithfully and unselfishly to the fact that God had put him there to meet that need. We reflect the image of God not only when we do something dramatic, but when we pay attention to what God has us doing every day and care for others we meet in quiet, practical, selfless ways.

Since we are God's image-bearers, all of our personal circumstances can be a way to participate in God's work. Instead of using our work to earn God's favor *or* to get all we can for ourselves, the gospel frees us to reflect our heavenly Father in his creative beauty, fruitful providence, and redemptive care. As we pursue our God-given work, whatever and wherever it might be, we participate in what God is doing in the world. In the church, God is creating a huge household of men and women who reflect his image and rely on his love and power in their relationships.

Our generous God invites us to reflect him in all we do. Daily he is using us as his image-bearers—participants in the coming kingdom—to bring him glory through this new economy, where all things are being brought under his righteous rule.

4 ORDINARY WORK, EXTRAORDINARY OPPORTUNITY

Most of the time our work, school, and family lives function on two levels. First, there is the immediate, surface level of following through on commitments and day-to-day issues of organizing, scheduling, producing, attending meetings, problem solving, etc. These responsibilities fill up most of our day, taking up much of our time, energy, talents, and attention. But ultimately they are all surface issues in that they are the things easiest to navigate and the activities in which we use our natural gifts and skills.

At a second deeper level of work, lie weightier issues of attitude and perspective. Here we encounter issues that burden and bring out the worst in us. These include getting along with others, forgiving sin, communicating, thinking the best of another, developing friendships, controlling personal jealousy, and using power and authority wisely. Unless we deliberately bring these issues into the light, most remain hidden while they shape and largely control our surface issues.

Here is an example showing this deeper, second realm:

Imagine yourself in a workplace discussion on how resources (time, money, etc.) should be applied to different departmental budgets. Based on past experience, you can predict how your peers will behave this time. Joe is hard to get along with because he tends to be brash and overly assertive. Pat usually loses out in these discussions because she avoids conflict and won't fight for what she thinks is best, even when she has excellent ideas. At the meeting you support Pat's good idea, but Joe becomes defensive. Later you get an e-mail from Joe stating that he has decided not to participate in a project with you because he is "too busy."

Let's summarize what is really happening here. Similar scenarios happen almost every day in workplaces, schools, churches, homes, and community groups.

1. What are some surface issues in this example?

- *How budget and company resources are distributed.*
- *How decisions are made.*
- *The work-flow process.*
- *Values and expectations for the way people treat one another in the office.*

2. What are some of the deeper issues?

- *Joe is overly assertive. His self-worth seems to come from being right and getting his way. He keeps a record of rights and wrongs.*
- *Pat is insecure about her role within the group and undervalues her own opinion, even when it is an excellent option.*
- *The decision-making process resembles that in a dysfunctional family rather than a rational discussion. Everyone is trying to please the boss. What is best for the group seems less important than winning.*
- *Joe is angry that he didn't get his way. He punishes you by withdrawing from a commitment. He does not consider what is best for the group or himself; he just punishes those who disagree.*

3. What are some gospel ways to move forward? (Think of how the image of God is or should be present in coworkers and processes.) There are things you can do one-on-one and in the group.

- *One-on-one, you can build relationships with Pat and Joe and encourage them to use the gifts God has given them. We should value ourselves (Pat) and others (Joe) as persons with dignity, made in the image of God, rather than obstacles to overcome, dominate, or win over.*

- *We should make decisions based on what is best for the group or institution rather than ourselves (Pat needs the courage to argue; Joe needs to renounce power plays.)*

- *You can encourage your boss to change the decision-making process by giving everyone a chance to speak; voting on things as a group; and having everyone explain why they believe their vote was best for the institution.*

Now try this with a challenging situation in your own workplace.

▶ What is the situation? Who are the people involved?

▶ What are the surface issues?

What creates tension and challenge in the situation, and how does each person (including you) respond to those challenges? How does each person's response make the situation better or worse?

▶ What are the deeper issues?

What fears, expectations, desires, and goals seem to shape each person's response (including yours) to the situation? How does that help you understand their surface responses?

▶ How should you interact with the situation as an image-bearer?

How can Jesus's work and presence in your life affect your own fears, expectations, desires, and goals? How will this change the way you participate in this situation?

▶ How can Jesus's desires for your coworkers help you move toward them with a desire to love, serve, and encourage them? How can you work together to do what is best for your institution?

5

A NEW ATTITUDE:
IMITATING GOD IN A WORLD OF WORK

BIG IDEA

As we saw in the last lesson, God gives men and women talents that can be used to reflect his image and character. Ultimately we offer ourselves to God's service to help bring the blessings of his kingdom into this world. The gospel makes us loved sons and daughters and changes our work from something we do for personal gain to something we do as *Imitators* of God who are eager to carry out his will.

5

EXTREME WORK:
STRIVING AND SLOTH

As God's image-bearers and imitators, we can only co-create. Farmers don't cause plants to grow, parents don't grow children from the dust of the ground, and scientists can't speak forth a new invention from nothing. We can't work on our own; we can't do what God does. God has chosen us to work "under" him to subdue the earth, fill it, and name his creatures. Our work, at its best, points back to God as a truer, greater, and eternal reality.

Our relationship to work has been marred by the fall. We see this in our attitudes. Rather than seeing work as something God has given us, we are prone to two opposite but equivalent errors: *striving* and *sloth*. Workaholics (the strivers) and slackers (the slothful) are controlled by fear, pride, and/or unbelief—rather than seeing themselves as imitators of God. The workaholic displays unbelief as he uses his work performance to justify himself internally or outwardly toward others. Pride and fear can motivate him to seek his identity in his work: pride, in that he wants an identity that he earns; fear, in that he doubts God will give him the identity he wants. Or he may fear that God doesn't love him enough to care for him at all. The slacker demonstrates unbelief and indifference to God by failing to use God's gifts for God's glory. He may be controlled by a fear of failure so that he is afraid to try meaningful work. Or he may have a sense of proud entitlement that doesn't believe he owes anything to God or anyone else—his priority is his own comfort.

The striver works for his own reputation, security, and gain instead of God's kingdom. The slothful person works for his own comfort instead of God's glory. Both striving and sloth reveal that our perspectives on God, identity, and work need realignment. Both reveal an absence of faith and love. And because both stem from unbelief, pride, and fear, we are vulnerable to both temptations at any given time.

STRIVING: WORK AS MASTER

Overwork places our need for comfort, control, security, and approval ahead of our relationship with God. The surface issue of overwork often flows from a deeper desire to control our circumstances instead of relying on God. This can be seen in a preoccupation with position and success as things that give us meaning and value. Our bent motivations shape our identity. Striving separates us from God's plan to make us more like Christ. God is always more concerned with our character than he is our competence, position, or productivity.

Instead of work being one part of life, we allow it to engulf things it should not. When having superior wealth, possessions, family, or reputation is an idol, our striving for more will come at a cost. It will destroy other things we value (wealth destroying family, or possessions harming reputation, etc.). When we misuse God's gifts of time, talent, and health, God's goal is to allow them to expose our idols so that we humbly return to him.

To this point, Jesus says to those who strive:

> "... do not be anxious about your life, what you will eat ... nor about your body, what you will put on. Is not life more than food, and the body more than clothing. ... O you of little faith! Therefore, do not be anxious, saying, 'What shall we eat?' or 'What shall we drink?' or 'What shall we wear?' For the Gentiles seek after all these things, and your heavenly Father knows that you need them all. But seek first the kingdom of God and his righteousness, and all these things will be added to you." (Matthew 6:25–34)

Fear, pride, or unbelief may functionally underlie our overwork, but each one also includes our failure to trust God in our circumstances.

SLOTH: WORK AS A CURSE

The opposite of striving is sloth, which views work as a curse to avoid. Often there is an underlying fear or unbelief about God's willingness to help with a difficult task, so a person prefers not to try and fail. Others feel they should not be expected to work.

When people feel they are being treated unfairly or feel the burden of work, they avoid or ignore it or put in minimal effort. Perhaps we don't view our work as something that intrinsically glorifies God; we'd rather serve ourselves with comfort or leisure. Those who struggle with sloth miss the truth that both work and leisure point to Christ's glory. That is why Paul reminds us to

> *Obey in everything those who are your earthly masters, not by way of eye-service, as people-pleasers, but with sincerity of heart, fearing the Lord. Whatever you do, work heartily, as for the Lord and not for men, knowing that from the Lord you will receive the inheritance as your reward. You are serving the Lord Christ. (Colossians 3:22–24)*

This side of heaven, we will always experience tension from life's competing priorities. As finite, fallen beings with limited time and resources, how else could we feel? The question we must ask is, When is "enough" work enough—and when is it not enough? Work gurus may talk about work-life balance, but such balance is technically impossible. Demands and circumstances change daily. We are always in flux, tempted to respond to the needs by changing our circumstances rather than understanding what God calls us to. Achieving balance can become our goal rather than seeing balance as a gift from God that comes from dependence on him to mediate the competing demands of life.

Our lack of balance can actually go even deeper. We may not technically overwork but still be enslaved to our jobs in our need for success. We may avoid sloth outwardly without serving Christ well. We might do a good job at a task, but it may be the wrong thing overall because we failed to love. We need the truth of the gospel and the power of the Holy Spirit to accurately understand our circumstances.

GOD-CENTERED WORK

Our culture urges us to be "balanced" by compartmentalizing—allocating so many hours to work, to family, to church, to leisure, etc. But eventually conflicts arise, and when the "margin" in one category disappears, it competes for the time and energy designated for other categories, producing guilt, frustration, anger, or paralysis. And simply trying to manage life's surface challenges differently doesn't address the idols that can operate even when we try to be "balanced."

Think of what happens when you encounter situations like these. Do you detect fear, pride, or unbelief in your attempts to address them?

- The boss demands that you work overtime on your spouse's birthday.
- You've just had a third child whose medical issues require hospitalization for the foreseeable future.
- You develop a medical condition that will affect your ability to do your job. Should you tell anyone at work?
- You want to move to a new area but cannot sell your home without losing a lot of money.

The quest for a "balanced" life puts each individual piece (your job, personal life, kids, parents, God, etc.) in competition with the rest. Your separate worlds never interact, and God isn't central to any of them. We move between different sets of expectations and values, forgetting that God created us to be whole people. Because we aren't integrated, we don't see that God desires to change us *as* we work or how he uses us in his kingdom *through* our work.

A more biblical solution is to think of our lives as spoked wheels with God as the hub. Everything takes its place as a spoke attached to the hub. If one spoke is detached, it may be a problem, but it is not catastrophic. God holds it all together. If one spoke can only carry a smaller load, the hub can guide the other spokes to absorb the stress. Keeping God at the center puts the events of life in proper perspective and helps us see that

God uses all things to make us more like Christ. God isn't relegated to one portion of life; he holds every part together.

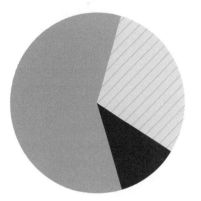 

To keep God as our hub, we may need to change our life patterns. At a deeper level, we may need to change what we think we "need" to do and our motivations for doing so (e.g., fear-based parenting, educational choices, keeping long work hours, meeting unspoken family expectations). How will we know we are doing the right things the right way? Friends can offer wisdom, but the ability to face the future without fear flows from trust in God as the mediator of our callings. And because God has promised answers when we seek his kingdom (Matthew 6:25–34), the answers will become clear in his time. As his children we can face the future without fear.

LIFE INTEGRATION DIAGNOSTIC

Beneath our tendencies toward striving and sloth are idolatries that can be dislodged by the Spirit as he exposes our hearts, leads us to truthful answers, and gives us the power to change. Ultimately we want Christ to rule our schedules, lives, motivations, and hearts.

First, list out your current life and work responsibilities as a pie chart. Then, ask yourself the following questions and discuss your answers with a trusted family member, coworker, or friend.

PIE CHART

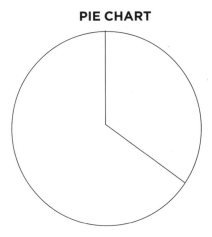

QUESTION SET 1

- How do I respond if I am criticized?
- What is my response when someone publicly critiques my work?

- How do I feel if someone overlooks my position or qualifications?
- What happens if I am not affirmed for the hours I spend at work?
- What if someone brings my competence, success, or ability into question?
- Which of these scenarios would get the biggest emotional response from me?

Do you see any pattern to your answers?

What might that pattern or system of beliefs be telling you?

QUESTION SET 2

- Do I waste time or "pretend" to work? How often do I do this?
- How much time do I spend pursuing get-rich-quick schemes?
- When was the last time I complained about not being respected or valued at work?
- Am I given enough resources to do my job? Am I underpaid for my work?
- Do I feel stuck in a dead-end position or lifestyle?
- Which of these thoughts would get the biggest emotional response from me? Why?

Do you see any pattern to your answers?

What might that pattern be telling you?

QUESTION SET 3

- To whom (or what) am I really entrusting my time? Future? Life?
- Is there anything underlying my answers in Question Sets 1 and 2 that makes me think I don't have options, so I have to put up with whatever situation my circumstances have placed me in?

- Am I giving my circumstances to God? Do I trust him to be the hub of my life, or am I giving him just a slice or two of my life's "pie"?

- What is more important to me: pleasing God with my work or pleasing people? Why is that?

- Do I trust God enough to let him disrupt my life if it enables me to know him more, serve others better, or honor those I love?

Finally redraw your life responsibilities below as a spoked chart—with Jesus at the hub. Ask him in prayer to become more of the hub this week.

SPOKED CHART

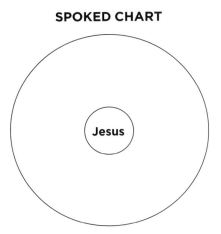

6 BOND-SERVANTS:
FROM SLAVES TO SONS AND DAUGHTERS

BIG IDEA

Some of us have been freed from a love of money, others from self-righteousness or self-importance, and others from self-hatred. We are all new people who owe our lives to Jesus. As we grow in our understanding of the gospel, we grow in gratitude and want to follow and worship the One who has given us new life! God doesn't treat us as workers, valued only for what we do, but as his sons and daughters, loved for who we are in Christ. What we do never defines who we are; our relationship to Jesus matters far more. Rather than our work being our identity, Jesus offers us true personhood as trusted sons and daughters in God's family.

THE FREEDOM OF SERVING GOD IN OUR WORK

The gospel frees us to not just "do the right thing" in our work, but also to genuinely love God and others. Even when we disagree with coworkers or know that what they are doing is wrong, we are still called to love them. Living with God at the center of our lives means that we aim at more than following a code of conduct; God wants us to reflect his character and love for others *while* we stand up for what is right.

How hard is that balancing act? It's impossible unless we are relying on God. We need to ask him for a grasp of his promises and power that overshadows our idols, fear of people, or the motivations and values of our workplaces. This will lead us to examine our hearts with questions like these:

- Where do I doubt that God is my true master at work and that he will take care of me? How is he calling me to be more open and loving with others instead of protecting my reputation or buckling under work pressures?

- Where do I struggle to believe that Jesus is enough for me? How do I need his help to resist the pressures of the crowd, even if it involves a loss of reputation or security? What price am I willing to pay for Christ to be seen in me? What is God calling me to in my current circumstances?

- In what ways do I try to look better than others? Am I too pre-occupied with following the rules? Do I look down on others who don't get it right? What does that reveal about my reliance on the righteousness of Christ?

- How do I need to trust Jesus in hard work situations? Do I trust him enough to let him transform me? We enter into Jesus's rest by trusting him, not ourselves. Then we receive the rest and freedom promised in the gospel.

God loved us when we were his enemies, and Jesus's work frees us from sin's power and changes us. Christ gives us the power to love all that he is—his truth, honesty, integrity, and goodness—and to become like him. He enables us to love others, seek their benefit, and even bless our enemies.

God's generosity toward us allows us to give more than what is required of us—to respond above and beyond in generosity toward others. To think more deeply about God's generosity to us, let's look at the origins of biblical servanthood in Deuteronomy 15:15–17 (NIV). This is the basis for understanding its fuller meaning in the New Testament.

> Remember that you were slaves in Egypt and the LORD your God redeemed you. That is why I give you this command today.
>
> But if your servant says to you, "I do not want to leave you," because he loves you and your family and is well off with you, then take an awl and push it through his ear lobe into the door, and he will become your servant for life. Do the same for your female servant.

The bond-servant allowed his master to pierce his earlobe with an awl (a small, pointed tool) against the door of the house. That's a very clear statement: by the power of blood you're permanently attached to this household and this master. As a mark of this bond, it was the custom to put in a gold earring after the awl was removed. With a simple voluntary act, the servant would be swearing by his own life-blood to never be free again (nor could he ever be sold).

These servants were no longer serving to pay a debt; rather, they desired to be members of the master's household who would be permanently cared for. As trusted parts of the household, these employees would usually be given stewardship over more of their master's affairs than typical servants. Although still servants, they were treated more like members of the family and given greater freedom, status, and responsibility.

The desire to become part of the master's household flowed from a love and understanding of the master's generosity. The freed man or woman who became a bond-servant experienced something so positive in the relationship that he or she was willing to put himself or herself at risk. When we experience true freedom in the gospel, our natural response is gratitude and a desire to serve the Master who pays our debts, puts his resources at our disposal, and gives us his family name.

As children who bear our Father's image and experience his acceptance, we should be even more compelled to serve others in God's household. Galatians 5:13 says that because of the gospel, we have new freedom in Christ, and we should use it as servants bound together in love. The gratitude for our freedom should compel us to become "enslaved" again, this time to be captured by our love for one another!

- At the cross we are truly accepted. We approach God as friends and sons, not as enemies. At the cross we are truly forgiven, for Christ paid the debt we could never pay ourselves. At the cross, we are made truly righteous; in exchange for our sin, Christ has given us his righteousness.

- Because we are loved as children and given the resources of our Father's household, we're free to pursue the things God loves, imitating him with honesty, justice, integrity, compassion, and generosity. Work flows from a grateful understanding of God's work on our behalf, leading us to love God by obeying his commands and working out his will.

- As bond-servants we treat the commands of our Master differently. His commands in Scripture are now our good guide. As we depend on the Spirit, our Father's commands show us how to live in love and true freedom. Becoming like Christ is not merely about sinning less, but about responding to God's grace to love others more.

- The gospel opens up the reality of life in the Spirit. Because the demands of the law have been met in Christ, we don't need to fear that God will reject us. Instead we are freed to use the abilities God has given us. Freedom, rather than guilt or duty, characterizes our daily lives.

In Mark 12:44 we see what it looks like to respond to God wholeheartedly. The poor widow completely trusts her Master to provide for her needs. Instead of giving a tenth of her income as commanded in Scripture, she gives all she has because she knows her Master is also her Father, who can and will take care of her. In Acts 4:36–37, Barnabas sold his property and gave the proceeds to the church. What compelled such extravagant action?

Finally, consider Paul, who in 1 Corinthians 9 lists the rights he has given up to share the gospel with the Corinthians without charge. Paul argued that he had a right to be paid but was under the Spirit's compulsion not to be. All believers should want to live with such passion and gratitude for Christ! We must rely on the Spirit to love as the whole law requires. When our words and actions are motivated by a passion for God, we find true joy and life.

All of us have seen wrongs plotted, displayed, and exalted. The Spirit will certainly lead us to avoid participating in those wrongs (and to repent of any we have committed). God's commands show us what he expects, but they are powerless to actually produce that obedience in us. The Spirit empowers our obedience, often asking us to step out in faith to go beyond what others would expect of us.

- An accountant who is asked to "cook" the books needs to do the right thing before God and care for others, which means putting himself at risk to speak the truth, protest the wrong, and refuse to cooperate for the sake of his coworkers and customers.

- The prosecutor who might naturally press for the maximum penalty so that he is seen as being tough on crime is confronted with a penitent defendant and realizes that mercy may also at times be required.

- The stay-at-home mom who is pressured to shun a mom whose children are out of control risks being shunned herself if she does the right thing by befriending the family.

- A student who is thinking of switching majors realizes that her career motivations are completely self-focused. She wonders if she should do something financially riskier that would require her to be more dependent on God.

What does our gratitude for Christ's love and our freedoms compel us to do? What do the commands of Scripture say you should *not* do, and what does the Spirit show you that love demands? Perhaps your dilemma involves a business deal, advertising campaign, or accounting practice; perhaps it involves how your children are treating a friend or an enemy. You may be aware of a fellow student who is cheating on exams under parental pressure to get good grades.

Whatever it is, the Spirit may be prodding you to do more than live for yourself and your own desires to be right, to be vindicated, or even to not get into trouble. The Spirit does not just teach our consciences right from wrong; he shows us how to rely on his power so that he can use us to re-create, change, redeem, and restore our broken world.

6

FROM WORK EXPECTATIONS TO LOVE COMMANDS

At work we can often be more concerned about staying out of trouble than about going beyond work expectations to love people as we've been loved by God. This exercise can help you move beyond pretending and performing to begin responding to relationships and circumstances with love. Perhaps the challenges of your workplace resemble the challenges of these examples:

- A stay-at-home mom might focus on a child's outward behavior rather than her heart attitude or disposition.

- A tired father might focus on enjoying himself, not making waves at home or with siblings, parents, and neighbors.

- Students might be focused on getting good grades at the expense of truly knowing a subject or topic. This might tempt them to cheat, cut corners, or overprepare in fear rather than to focus on knowledge and its application.

- A salesman may focus his energy on trashing his competition with innuendo and gossip rather than communicating honestly about the strengths and limitations of his company's products or services.

The challenges faced by these people—and perhaps you—are to move beyond the basics of "work expectations" to a willingness to love as Christ has loved us.

Think of your own example here and ask yourself:

- What are the expectations placed on me in my work environment?
- How am I called to love God and others better in my specific circumstances?

In the coming week, reflect daily on how you looked at the issues and circumstances using the chart below. To begin, move from column 1 to column 2 to column 3 and ask yourself, What if my expectations for my day changed so that my number-one job was to love God and the people around me in this particular circumstance (versus just doing the basics of my job)? What would be different?

Situation	What my job expects	What a love for God and others might require beyond what my job expects
Example	Possible Responses	Possible Responses
A teammate, family member, or close friend makes a mistake	I help the company succeed, so I might address the situation but also cover it up. I make my opinion known first to my teammate and then my boss if needed (to shade things so I look best). I come up with the best way to fix mistakes (and highlight my own abilities).	I speak up, knowing I'm also prone to make mistakes, yet God still loves me. I work with my teammate to help him as opposed to scoring points. I'm concerned about how a mistake could harm customers or someone else; I don't just fix it to move on. When tempted to judge a teammate's negligence, I remember that Christ has established my record and does not shame me or judge my competency.

Situation	What my job expects	What a love for God and others might require beyond what my job expects

7

STEWARDS:
SERVING JESUS BY SERVING OTHERS

BIG IDEA

Every opportunity that enters our lives is given by God. He wants us to represent him in ways that bring him glory and impact others with good works and the gospel. The Greek word for *Steward* is closely tied to the idea of being an agent—someone who is given resources and opportunities to carry out someone else's mission and purposes. Today, this idea lies behind the work of real estate agents, insurance agents, and secret agents. These modern stewards are equipped to act within a specific context to promote the interests of a known other.

We respond to the circumstances God gives us in ways that either conform to God's will or are opposed to it. God's provision for us as his children transforms our orphan attitudes about resources like time and money to uncover ways to seek the good of others with everything he has entrusted to us, in service to our Savior.

7

TWO ASPECTS OF STEWARDSHIP

The gospel changes our outlook to help us serve others as Jesus has served us. We do this for God's glory and for others. We can love and serve others unconditionally because we've been loved and served that way ourselves. We work out of gratitude for Jesus and his love, but more than that, Jesus says that we serve and care for him when we serve others in his name (Matthew 10:42, Mark 9:41).

There are many implications to this spiritual reality. In a gospel-centered community, businesspeople compete knowing that other suppliers are not the enemy and customers are not pawns for personal gain. Advertisers make claims about products in the context of honest relationships with consumers. Housewives love their families despite trying circumstances. Students acknowledge exams as legitimate judges of what they know, and trust God for their success. This serving out of a knowledge and trust of God is what the New Testament calls being a *diakonos* or steward. Stewards carry out the will of an authority, who has a vision for a long-term plan of action. Our actions are not our own as stewards; they are submitted to the Lord to bring about his purposes in history.

At age twenty, Wendy Clark started Carpe Diem Cleaners. Initially her goal as a Christian businessperson was to earn profits that would go to cross-cultural missions. Several years into her career, Jesus helped her to see that her business *itself* was a ministry, a service to God and her community. Now she goes to work knowing that she is serving God, not only by giving money away, but by serving her clients and employees. This has radically changed her business, particularly her focus on her employees, mostly Latino moms. Wendy offers them flexible work schedules that respect their callings as wives and moms.

Carpe Diem's hours accommodate their schedules "so that they aren't stressed out trying to get their kids to school, running late to work, and getting home on time." She changed the format of her service education events by taking the women—and their kids—to a family camp in the country. That way she gets everyone's full attention while the families get a vacation they probably wouldn't have had otherwise. She serves not just her employees, but their whole households.[3]

The gospel enables us to repent from seeing ourselves as orphans—as those who are abandoned and without resources—so that we can look beyond ourselves and see others as God has made them. When we rest in our status as God's beloved children we flourish, and the communities where God has placed us are impacted by our service. The gospel helps us repent of the self-centeredness that might have taken the resources entrusted to us and used them for ourselves. Instead, we invest our time, energy, and relationships for the sake of the kingdom.

In Colossians 4:7, Paul calls Tychicus both a faithful steward (*diakonos*) and bond-servant (*doulos*). Here is the connection: bond-servants love God with their heart, soul, mind, and strength. All the love they have come to know is returned to God in worship and in service to others. Our relationship to and reliance on Jesus is a prerequisite for serving neighbors in his name. "Bond-service" is the Godward component, based on the Father's love for us. It fuels the neighborly "stewardship" component, which is our service for God toward others.

Our union with Jesus is foundational for serving our neighbors. He must oversee and empower our stewardship and also be the reason we serve. When we love our neighbors, our service is transformed into worship in gratitude for all Christ has done. Just as we see in the story of the sheep and the goats (Matthew 25:31–46) and in Colossians 3:22–24, Jesus is the

---

3. Adapted from Amy Sherman, http://www.crosswalk.com/family/career/vocational-stewardship-for-the-common-good.html and www.carpediemcleaning.com/mission-vision/.

ultimate recipient of our work, which is a great spiritual encouragement if our desire is to glorify him.

There are two ways our stewardship is reflected in relationships to neighbors.

Stewards are sent into daily life as God's agents. God has placed us where we live, like the man Jesus healed in Mark 7, to be his hands and feet, his eyewitnesses, and his voice. We are to be salt and light in the world, to preserve its good and expose its evil so people can repent and turn to Christ. As stewards, we dedicate our work to the love of neighbor and the advancement of God's kingdom.

Don Flow, CEO of Flow Motor Corporation in Winston-Salem, North Carolina, desired to honor God in his business. This led him to sell cars at a fixed price and to focus on service and long-term relationships with his customers.

"Doing what I am doing was as natural for me as a pastor being called to preach in the pulpit," Don says. "Loving that person that walks beside you is just an abstraction—I knew lots of Christians who talked about love all the time and they were horrible to work with. This is like a complete anomaly.

"I have this passion to make it real in practice—I'm not talking about preaching to those who work for me, to customers or others. I'm not talking about favoring Christians who work here. I want to respect and value all people, regardless of their beliefs. But I am talking about living out the implications of what I believe. This is reflected in how we treat people, what our practices are, and what we think is important."[4]

Stewards are sent by God to our neighbors. As we love our neighbors, eventually they may see that God is caring for them through us. When we share the gospel verbally, they may come to know Jesus's love and respond in faith. Stewards recognize that there are no ordinary people; all bear the image of God. God gives us all we have to glorify him by loving our neighbors and bringing the gospel to bear on their lives.

---

4. http://ethix.org/2004/04/01/ethics-at-flow-automotive.

"I really owe so much of the health of this business to my coworker and COO Jill Evans," said Trupoint President Matt Lievens at a breakfast meeting. "I used to go about my day making decisions in response to events and situations, rarely thinking about the people involved. But Jill regularly asks us to look at things from another perspective—to 'see' people in their unique circumstances. She quietly asks, 'I wonder what must be happening over at their shop for them to be responding to us like this? What chaos must be causing them to tyrannize us?' in response to some emergency.

"The light goes on for just a few minutes and we think about their boss, or the pressure they have after some business failure. It often softens us and causes us to be gentler as we enter conflict or some difficult negotiation. In seeing people, Jill tries to 'see' the desires that motivate them. 'What do they want?' Jill would say. We talk about their futures and ask, 'Who they could be? What are they good at?' We try to see how they might be trapped by their fears. She has introduced a whole new world of thinking about people. I am deeply indebted to her. In helping us see ourselves as servants of those around us, she has changed our whole model of business."

Some people seek ways to publicly serve God, but if we take the parable of the sheep and the goats (Matthew 25:31–46) seriously, the indirect and hidden ways of serving others are truly Christian work. We may be very surprised on the last day as we see God honor the small things done with great love, hidden from the world's eyes but performed faithfully in response to Jesus. Jesus wants to meet us in our work in ways we cannot anticipate. He meets us in the people around us to accomplish his purposes in our lives and theirs. Asking for the knowledge of his presence and discernment of our circumstances is critical to living faithfully each day.

Interruptions from difficult and unlovable coworkers, bosses, clients, students, patients, children, and relatives give us a chance to practice repentance and faith. When we are given grace to see our orphan self-centeredness, the Spirit gives us grace to repent and step out in faith, to love as God has loved us. The irritations and stressors we once avoided or overcame in the least painful way now become opportunities to serve Christ and repent of sin. The relationships of our workplace are one of the "chief laboratories of the gospel" where God is glorified as we are refined and transformed.

lesson

7

MY AGENDA, GOD'S AGENDA

This exercise builds on the previous lesson's exercise. ***From Work Expectations to Love Commands*** encouraged you to look back on your day and reflect on the motivations you had amid the chaos of daily life. This time we would like you to *anticipate* and ask God to show you what he might have in store for you each day.

Start by writing a "To-Do" list at the beginning of each day. Review that list in the evening and write down what God *actually* had for you that day.

In addition, create a "Done-For" list of the ways God worked through others to serve you as his beloved child.

Repeat the exercise by writing a new list each day.

Every morning use your list to turn your priorities over to God. Each evening think about how your "To-Do" and "Done-For" lists lead you to a changed perspective and growth in gratitude during the course of the week.

1. What did God do within my heart, soul, and mind as the week progressed?

2. What do these lists reveal about my thoughts about stewardship? How can God use the opportunities in my life to grow me in service to others? What are some specific changes I now know I can make?

3. How do your "To-Do" and "Done-For" lists reveal how you think about your week and God's purposes for you?

TO DO

Example: Please help me in my attitude toward my coworker Jamie. He can push my buttons with his self-centeredness and whining. Help me not to lose my patience with him again.

DONE FOR

Example: Father, thanks for helping me see Jamie in a new way today. Because you prompted me to ask a few questions, I was able to really listen when he talked about his wife's chronic illness and his college son's poor life choices. That really helps me see him as a fellow struggler, instead of an annoyance. Forgive me for my lack of love, and help me to know how to love him better.

TO DO	DONE FOR
Date	Date
Date	Date
Date	Date
Date	Date

8 AMBASSADORS:
REPRESENTATIVES SENT BY GOD

BIG IDEA

We are people who were once separated from God; now we represent him as we go to others with the good news of Jesus. Because we've been loved so well, as we go, we put aside our own goals and embrace our calling to extend God's kingdom, resting in God's provision, authority, and power. When we view life and work through gospel lenses, we see our neighbors as God sees them—broken people who need Jesus as much as we do.

BECOMING AMBASSADORS

The story of Jonah is one of the Bible's best examples of someone called by God to go to others radically different from himself. When God called Jonah, a prophet in Israel, to preach repentance to Israel's enemies, Jonah wasn't just reluctant, he ran in the opposite direction (Jonah 1:3). Left to our own resources, we might not run physically like Jonah, but our hearts can be just as hard to the needs of those who aren't like us. Jonah resented God for sending him to strangers as an ambassador of welcome, peace, forgiveness, and repentance.

When we work with others whose methods are drastically different from ours or with those who actively oppose us, we are confronted, like Jonah, with our own selfishness and self-protection. But our new identity in Christ dismantles our fears and biases and gives us a heart to love others. In the New Testament, Jesus tells us that the "sign" of Jonah (Luke 11:29–32) is repentance from hard-heartedness.

God often allows perceived competitors, enemies, and strangers to cross our paths so that we are confronted with our personal guardedness, self-righteousness, and judgment. God wants us, like the Good Samaritan, to choose hospitality rather than isolation. It is too easy to limit our close relationships to those who are like us, who unwittingly reinforce our perceptions of life and rarely challenge our assumptions. In Jonah's case, God sent sailors, a storm, and a huge fish to deliver him from his hard-heartedness toward the Ninevites. Through his testing, Jonah came to know the true character of God as well as his inability to repent in his own strength.

In our work it can be easy to give in to temptations like the following rather than work toward mutual understanding and hospitality:

- In our weakness it is tempting to judge and slander our perceived competitors in a short-sighted way to win others over.

- In our self-righteousness we can treat frustrating coworkers harshly or treat peers with superiority and contempt.

- In our perceived powerlessness it can be easy to gossip about those we consider foolish, out of touch, or selfish in their decision making.

Just like Jonah we need the power and resources promised in the gospel to help us repent of our foolishness and rely completely on Christ's work. He is the only One with the power to give us significance and free us from seeking life and meaning outside the truth of the gospel.

- Instead of competing with others, feeling discouraged when we don't measure up and judgmental when we do, the Holy Spirit gives us the peace, confidence, and integrity to promote the accomplishments of others, even those of our competitors.

- Instead of being discouraged when our approval-seeking coworkers thrive (and internally glad when they fail), the Spirit gives us the power to cheer on their successes and mentor them quietly in their failures. Our security lies in Jesus, not our personal record.

- Instead of pursuing power through gossip and slander, the gospel frees us to see that our lives and careers are secure in the powerful hands of Jesus.

The truth of the gospel helps us remember that there are no circumstances we encounter that are not for our good or God's glory. His Spirit gives us the power to resist sin and pursue peace and blessing in every relationship and circumstance.

Our grasp of what Jesus's righteous record means has another effect on our being ambassadors in our work. If we are secure in our relationship with Jesus, we are free to spend time with those around us, regardless of their position, background, or beliefs. Rather than worry about what it will look like if we hang out with a certain subset of people in our workplace, the gospel opens us up to moving freely among different groups and personalities. Because we are confident of who we are in Christ, we no longer need to maneuver our relationships to get ahead or avoid people because of their reputation. We are free to care for strangers and outsiders because we understand what it is to be loved as a stranger— even while an enemy!

God's love displayed through Jesus compels us to love others well. The reality that God goes before us in all our relationships frees us to establish meaningful connections built on genuine love and care with coworkers. We don't see them as an evangelistic project—something that can be much more about us than them. It is the Holy Spirit's job to convict and transform hearts, not ours. Our calling is to pursue authentic relationships, to be available to love as we've been loved.

Part of being a true ambassador is to know and be known by those around us, just as we know and are known by God himself. We've been entrusted with time, talent, and resources to move toward others, not protect ourselves in fear. We relate authentically because we've been freed by Jesus to love as we are loved.

Being gospel-centered also changes the tenor and tone of our conversations. The gospel helps us understand what it is to be other-centered. If we are worried about what others think of our outlook on life or our personal record of sin, we can unwittingly build walls by what we say, instead of building a bridge toward greater understanding. Our main job as ambassadors is to be in relationships with those in whom God is already at work, seeking to discover what he is doing in their hearts. So don't worry about your reputation or about letting others know where you or the Bible stand on a particular subject. If they want to know more, they will ask.

Instead of worrying about yourself, ask questions. Ambassadors care more about the needs of others rather than about being cared for themselves. Jesus has already done, and is doing, that for us! If we get to know others and love them well, they will respond when they see the ways they've been loved.

The power of the gospel is displayed when we welcome others who are outside of Christ. Our welcome communicates how much we enjoy them. Our words, nonverbal cues, and tone tell others clearly and quickly whether they are valued or merely tolerated. God's love is a welcoming love; it embraces the outsider, forgives the rebel, and is long-suffering and merciful to the prodigal. God's love is the kind of love we want to imitate and communicate. We imitate it because we know it personally, and we communicate it when it overflows from our lives. Our thoughts, actions, and words will always reflect where we place our hope and how God has impacted (or failed to impact) us.

When we welcome others, do we treat them as befits their eternal nature—with dignity, care, and grace as those made in the image of God? Treating people with honor and respect—the way we would want to be treated ourselves—is an intensely biblical practice based on our own knowledge of being created in the image of God. That should get noticed in a world bent on proving itself and getting all it can! It should encourage us that, even in our failures, God has us right where he wants us. As we serve him there, he is interceding for us (John 17:15).

A life in which repentance is normal and genuine allows us to be authentic with believer and unbeliever alike. If we can admit we're not perfect and demonstrate that we're approachable and nondefensive because God is helping us in our struggles, the gospel becomes so much more accessible to those who don't know him. Isn't it the essence of the good news that there is hope for sinners like us? Jesus goes before us, interceding and providing so that we can be ambassadors who make the most of every opportunity to love others well.

lesson

EXERCISE

PEOPLE OF PEACE AND HOSPITALITY

Make a list of the people from your workplace who might have a hard time getting along with you or that have an ongoing conflict with you. Try to describe the problem from their point of view.

Now, make a second list of people you have a hard time getting along with in your workplace. Do you notice any envy, judgment, coldness, etc., in your attitude because of comparisons (of superiority or criticism) you have made about that person? How would you compare the two lists? List what you need to receive from Christ to let go of your sinful reactions and reach out to the other person.

How can you rely on Jesus as you become more of a person of peace and hospitality? As you repent of things on your second list, consider pursuing one or two of the people on that list with kindness, reconciliation, and relationship. Think about the gifts and interests you might have in common. Could you work on a project together or collaborate on a common goal? (Having said that, please know that some relationships need to be mended by someone else because of the depth of pain and hurt that exists. That's okay. God is capable of calling someone else into that relationship if he desires to see change in those cases. Every human need is not a call from God!)

9

MESSENGERS:
GOD EQUIPS US
WITH THE GOSPEL

BIG IDEA

God has entrusted us with our relationships. He has enlisted us as his *Messengers* in a mission to share the gospel with and make disciples of our children, friends, neighbors, and coworkers. In the past he used others to free us from our rebellion and to disciple us in the faith. Now he invites us to do the same in partnership with his Spirit. So, rather than being consumed by our personal agendas, the Spirit helps us to see that our lives are full of opportunities to share the good news with those who do not know Christ.

A NEW OUTLOOK ON NEIGHBORS

Sharing our faith doesn't have to be offensive to be effective. No one wants to be *that* guy! When we tell others about the impact of the good news on our lives, we're reminded that, just like us, other people want to be loved authentically, listened to, and respected for their point of view. We can do that! We've seen that God has placed us where we are to be his image-bearers, imitators, bond-servants, stewards, and ambassadors. As we interact with others and plant the seeds of the gospel, the Spirit does the work of transformation. We just need to be a faithful presence that points to his work and simply tells our story of faith when others ask about the reason for the hope we have.

Step into the hall or aisle at work and notice the people around you. Whom do you know? How can you get to know them better? Take it all in. Give thanks for this place, including the pleasures, the pains, the friends, and even those who call you their enemy. Jesus has sent you as a gospel messenger into your workplace "neighborhood" so that he can give sight to the blind, freedom to captives, and new life to the condemned. Does that feel like good news to you? Does it bring you joy or do you feel guilty for not doing more? Your workplace relationships are entrusted to you by God. Enjoy them! When we lose ourselves in thanks for God's purposes, we find a deep contentment that comes from his Spirit. Getting lost in the grand cause of God, we're finally able to forget ourselves and live.

Whether you are a stay-at-home mom, student, contractor, or office worker, it's no accident that God has placed you near your coworkers. Their proximity is a great relationship builder. When my family moved to our current neighborhood, we purposely purchased a home on a corner lot with a detached garage. We wanted more sidewalk so we could meet and greet neighbors. We tore down the privacy fence and built a deck close to the street. We put a workshop in the garage, where people could see us working on projects that became conversation starters. In my previous job I took an office where coworkers could easily drop by in the course of the day. I chose to work at a round, more collaborative conference table rather than a desk.

Modern life is often described as crowded loneliness, where we move from dehumanizing work environments to cocooned home environments. I wanted to offer a different model, an environment built on trust-building and face-to-face conversation. You might have an attached garage or live in an apartment building—that's not the point here. Thinking of creative ways to pursue hospitality (1 Timothy 3:2) and establish personal connections is part of what it means to love others for Christ's sake.

We need to think about how and when to present the gospel, especially in today's workplace, which (rightly) frowns on proselytizing "on the clock." We need to use our lunch hours, after-work hours and home life to share life with coworkers. Remember, we are not called to bring people to Jesus so much as we are to bring Jesus to people through authentic lives and a welcoming attitude built on how Christ welcomes and accepts us. We're told to be ready to give a word when asked to do so (1 Peter 3:14–18). If we are in relationship with those around us but doing life differently, people *will* ask! Saint Francis said, "Preach the gospel at all times and when necessary use words." It isn't merely our words that have power; it is the gospel at work under our words that makes them powerful and effective when we have opportunity to use them.

You may have pretty good reasons for hesitating about using words. Many of us have stumbled through or listened to gospel presentations that were impersonal, careless, self-righteous, dehumanizing, sometimes burden-inducing rather than burden-lifting. It doesn't have to be that way if your life is a reflection of Christ's life and a signpost for the gospel. When people are welcomed and they compare how you treat them to the way unbelievers treat them, they will see the difference Jesus has made in your life. They will want it for themselves and say, "Tell me more!"

True, our actions may not always be interpreted correctly. Sometimes people might react negatively for reasons of their own. Others might say, "Wow, you are a fantastic guy!" and you might need to respond, "Well, actually I'm not. I just have a great Savior." At those moments, when the Spirit is at work, our words need to be purposeful and direct. We need to use clear and simple language and stories that others understand.

I grew up reading books on apologetics, but after sharing the gospel with others over the last twenty years, I now think that few people come to faith through rational arguments alone. Their questions demand answers, but they come to faith when God reaches their hearts as well. Much of the current generation is skeptical of organized religion and antagonistic toward God. For them, reason alone is not enough. Truth also needs to pass the "smell" test, where people see if your way of life matches up to their life experience. This is where our lives make a critical difference. Spiritual decisions are usually not made quickly but over time, in relationship. This makes relationships vital but tricky since the current generation is hungry for face-to-face relationship but because of technology is isolated, ill-equipped, and fearful to engage in authentic connections.

To relate well to those around us, we need to free ourselves of religious jargon. Good friends over the past ten years have helped me get rid of "insider" language to explain how I relate to God ("sharing your faith," "giving my testimony," "got saved," "sanctification, justification," etc.). If you're like me, you've probably spent a lot of time inside Christian circles. It might take a lot of work to relate to people outside of them. Think about telling your story in a new way. Are you authentic? Is life all roses? How well does your story match your current life circumstance? How is God freeing you from a bent toward serving yourself today? How is the good news good for *you* today? Can you communicate with others without using a lot of theological terms that are only understood in a church subculture?

Second, when you show up, ask good questions. If you want to care for people, don't wait for an invite; go and build relationships. Invite others into your world so they see how faith is a real alternative to the crazy ways the world lives. When people recognize that you care, they will respond positively. If they sense they are your project, they won't stick around long. Visit a coworker when he is in the hospital, bring a meal, offer to drive a neighbor's kids home from school. Love others in simple, practical ways, and build relationships that are truly concerned about their lives. The Spirit-prompted conversations will follow when they are ready.

Third, after establishing relationships, be creative in getting to know your coworkers better. Hobbies, shared projects, community initiatives, meals, celebrations, even shared vacations are ways to spend time with them. I am a big fan of multi-tasking; getting to know someone doesn't need to take a lot of extra time. When you are performing tasks, going to meals, or getting a job done, do it with someone else. Ask your peers for their perspective on subjects—and listen. Let them at some point *ask* you for yours. Instead of doing the church-based youth program with your son or daughter, consider joining one at the YMCA or YWCA, Boy and Girl Scouts, etc. Throw your lot in with unbelievers and be a witness to what God wants to do (and is doing) in your workplace. Some of the best conversations I've had with unbelievers occurred when I wasn't looking for them, when others asked me for my take on the meaning, purpose, and direction of life.

Shared life circumstances are great for interacting about age and stage issues as well. Have coworkers over. Throw a party for your work team at the end of a significant project. Never go to lunch alone. Carpool. Hang out with a coworker or client on a business trip. Affirm someone in your workplace for his hard but necessary work.

Finally, pray that God would show you what he is doing, how he is going before you and spiritually pacing your relationships. Pray that he would show you the right time to start a relationship, enter into a conversation, push for more depth beyond surface interaction, and the time to encourage a decision to follow Christ. He has placed you where you are to let the message of the gospel impact your relationships with believers and unbelievers—and he is overseeing those relationships for your good and his glory.

9

EXERCISE

A LIFESTYLE OF LOVE

Think about the people you encounter at work in a typical day or week. Make a list of them now. Next, ask God to show you ways you can be more purposeful in connecting with those people. Write those down. Ask God to show you how he wants you to sow, water, or harvest in your words and actions. Think of "sow, water, and harvest" as First, Second and Third Steps like these:

First Steps: Getting to know the person to understand who he or she is.

Second Steps: Sharing more about yourself and your life in honest, transparent ways.

Third Steps: Introducing or following up on spiritual topics in a conversational, nonthreatening way.

Remember, it is God's Spirit who reaches a person's heart and enables him or her to see his or her need and to trust in Christ.

Let's work through a couple of examples.

Name	First, Second, Third Steps	Content of Conversation
1. Jeanine, Coworker	First	Go to lunch for birthday celebration
2. Joe, Custodian	Second	Follow up on conversation about parents
3. Sal, Customer	Second	Ask about movie with spiritual themes
4. Joan, Divorced teammate	Third	Inquire about last week's sadness

Try it with people you know from your workplace.

Name	First, Second, Third Steps	Content of Conversation
1.		
2.		
3.		
4.		
5.		

10

EVERYDAY SABBATH:
RESTING FOR WORK *AND* LEISURE

BIG IDEA

Work and leisure are good gifts from God, but they can become idols that pull us from him. In this lesson, we'll look at how a gospel-centered pursuit of rest brings work and leisure back under the authority of God. If we aren't regularly setting aside time for God and his people, our free time can be eaten up in purposeless entertainment and recreation, where we amuse ourselves in self-indulgence. The gospel turns us from self-centered uses of both work and leisure to embrace a genuine *Sabbath* rest.

SPIRITUAL REST:
HOW THE GOSPEL HELPS US UNPLUG

How rested are you? Many of us spend our time running from one activity to another without ever experiencing true rest for our souls. Work, leisure, activities with our kids, and constant communication with people add up to a frenetic lifestyle. We just can't seem to unplug.

Perhaps rest seems out of reach for you. But Jesus does promise us rest. He says to us, "Come to me, all who labor and are heavy laden, and I will give you rest" (Matthew 11:28). This gospel-powered rest comes from the sure knowledge that our sins are forgiven, that Jesus has done the work of salvation for us, that we can stop our striving for perfection, meaning, being right, and getting ahead, and instead turn to Jesus and trust him for all these things. True Sabbath rest flows from our relationship with Christ. He is our rest and peace.

It's easy for us to lose focus on our relationship with Christ as we go through our week. When that happens, we see some of the following things take over our lives:

- Our work becomes our identity instead of being God's dearly loved child.
- We can't stop working because "It's all up to us." We don't remember that our heavenly Father is our true provider.
- Even when we set aside time to rest, we can't stop doing. Our minds never stop thinking, planning, etc.
- We would rather do almost anything (send e-mails, text, talk on the phone, watch TV or sports, shop, etc.) than spend time with Jesus.

- Gathering to celebrate with God's people on Sundays becomes just one more option on a long list.

All of this reflects how well we know Jesus and how thoroughly his love has taken over our hearts and lives. To know that God is for us, that he loves and cares for us enough to take our death and give us his life, is what leads us to true spiritual rest. But without a grasp of the gospel, what we do during leisure times and Sundays will be, at best, just a temporary diversion from work.

Spiritual rest is completely different from work and leisure. Knowing Jesus and his rest transforms both our work and our leisure. When we encounter Jesus, it leads to a repentance and renewal that helps us become God-centered and other-centered in both our work *and* leisure. When pursued regularly as a way to connect to God and neighbor, spiritual rest can reshape all our other activities to reflect the truths of the gospel. For those who pursue work and leisure without God, there is no true rest. But for those who seek God as the source of spiritual rest, every day can be a day of rest.

Spiritual rest is modeled and empowered by Jesus. In the Gospels, Jesus takes time for both work and leisure. He feeds the five thousand, parties with tax collectors, yet also takes time to rest, pray, and be with his disciples—a time that is neither work nor leisure (Luke 4:42; 5:16; 6:12; 9:28; Matthew 14:23; Mark 1:35; 14:32–34). In those times he relates to his heavenly Father and shows his disciples the power of being in God's presence. He is God, yet as a man he meets with his Father to give us a model and example. He refuses to let work or leisure dictate his choices, and when those forces overwhelm his disciples, he models a deliberate retreat to counteract their power. When we pursue spiritual rest, we position ourselves to drink deeply of grace, even in the midst of busy lives. Spiritual rest happens when we stop relying on our own efforts and depend fully on Jesus (Hebrews 4). In so doing, our work is aligned to his work, and he is able to work through us.

Pursuing spiritual rest reminds us that we have a good Father. When we center our lives on *our* work and *our* leisure, we are easily confused by what we think we have earned for ourselves and what God has given us. When we let ourselves be pursued by Jesus, work and leisure lose their power to shape us. When we pursue spiritual rest, we realize that we bring nothing to God, yet we can expect everything from him. We have nothing to offer that we have not been given; we offer ourselves only as broken vessels for God to use. When Jesus removed himself from daily life, he taught his disciples to pray to his heavenly Father. He taught them to pray for and give thanks for simple things like daily bread, to ask for forgiveness and to forgive others. He showed his disciples how to be vigilant against temptations in the worlds of work and leisure and how to pursue God's kingdom as the alternative to their seductive power (Matthew 6:5–15). This is a lifestyle of every day rest in God's provision, love, and care. It's an each-and-everyday lifestyle of turning from our own pursuits and placing ourselves under God's care and protection.

A weekly Sabbath changes our perspective on work and leisure. Several years ago I began to radically unplug myself from my daily patterns for one day in seven. This is a hard task and I fail much more than I succeed, but it is an important practice nonetheless. Here's how I have decided to implement this in my life: I worship with God's people; I try to avoid both work and entertainment-oriented leisure in order to rest; I pursue relationship with God; and I spend time with people who love God. You may have other ways of pursuing a Sabbath rest one day a week.

Think about some additional ways you can actively pursue and enter into rest communally with other believers or your family.

By setting one day a week aside to focus on my relationship with God and others, I'm better able to reflect on the week that has passed and dedicate the week ahead to God. I'm better able to spend time in the Word and prayer, to remind myself of the gospel and repent where I need to. Even when imperfectly pursued, this practice has renewed me. When I set aside time during a particularly difficult day or week, in the midst of overwhelming demands placed on me by myself or others, it is easier to see how those demands are transformed by the pursuit of God's kingdom. When I am tugged to plug back in—out of fear that I won't measure up or achieve some goal—I can see more clearly the false, idolatrous expectations of work and leisure. Even in my failure God is at work, and I can more easily repent of those failures the next time they intrude on God's priorities because I see them more clearly. A similar thing happens when I take time for a deliberate yearly vacation from work, attend a conference or retreat, or spend time with family to allow God to clarify my priorities.

A rhythm of spiritual rest transforms our outlook on life. Even though we set aside one day a week for worship and rest, every day has the potential to be a Sabbath to the Lord. Spiritual rest in all its forms (daily, weekly, seasonal, and annual) helps us return to our work with a renewed perspective on "the daily grind" as something more—an act of worship in Jesus's presence. When Jesus declared that he was Lord of the Sabbath, he was acknowledging that he was doing his Father's work. He created and re-created, healed and celebrated, to bring sinners into the rest and worship of God (Matthew 12:1–16). Sabbath is more than the absence of work; it is a reliance on God to give up our own agendas and enter into the work he has set before us and to do it in his strength rather than our own (John 5:19). In one sense, we have nothing to do but receive each day's work as a gift from him. As we receive that work as a gift from God, we are sent out into mission, and he goes before us and with us. God longs to work in us and through us if we would only be strong enough to be weak and let him (Philippians 2:13)! Worship helps us to live our lives by faith in Jesus, who loves us and gave himself up for us (Galatians 2:20).

We don't observe spiritual rest to prove that we are God's redeemed people. We pursue spiritual rest *because* we are God's beloved children. When we celebrate being in his presence, we are reminded of our participation in his work to reclaim the world for him. Jesus's finished work is the truest place of rest for us as believers. The Sabbath celebrates the security of our relationship with God, God's future final victory over sin and death, and his sure return. Our personal priorities in work and our "need" for leisure are diminished when we see how our fears dominate our appetites and attention at God's expense. And when we repent of our fears, Jesus is better able to work in us and through us.

So the secret to true spiritual rest is to stop depending on our own actions and to depend instead on Jesus. When we connect with him, give up our striving, and take on his work, we're able to pursue real rest. As we experience his presence, we will come to know true Sabbath rest throughout our lives. Burdens are lifted and idols dethroned when we let the Spirit displace the things that have tried to rule us, and we plead instead for Jesus to fill us and work through us.

lesson

EXERCISE

BRINGING SABBATH REST INTO EVERY DAY OF THE WEEK

The patterns of the fall have become embedded in work and leisure. These forces want us to be shaped into their image rather than the image of God.

▶ What are some things that distract you when you pursue spiritual rest? *(checking e-mail or social media posts, turning on a ball game, housecleaning, etc.)*

▶ What might lie underneath those patterns? Why do you allow them to distract? *(What, at the heart level, keeps you choosing other things over Jesus when actively pursuing spiritual rest?)*

Now consider what false beliefs (about God and you) are beneath your actions.

▶ What falsehoods about God's care for you and the identity he has given you reinforce the choices and patterns that keep you from spiritual rest?

85

▶ What truths of the gospel do you need to believe instead?

For example, someone might say, "I have a really hard time not compulsively checking my e-mail at night and on Sundays. My coworkers all do it and expect me to do the same, so I don't want to be the 'slacker' on the team. So, in a very real sense, 'who others say I am' (a slacker, someone who isn't dedicated, someone who might someday be 'off' the team) matters more to me than who God says I am. It also makes me feel important—like they just can't get things done without me."

In contrast, God says I matter not because of what I do but because of what Jesus has already done. God is my fortress and my protector. He delivers me from the idolatry of success or acceptance (Psalm 31). *Jesus* establishes my "rightness" before God (Philippians 3:8–10), not my accomplishments or achievements.

"When I really believe that, it empowers me to trust God and 'put down' my work to deliberately rest in him as my Spiritual Rest. Those promises also remind me that it's okay to tell my coworkers that I don't read e-mail so that I can focus on my spiritual life and value my family. If it's truly urgent, they should call me and I'll get back to them as soon as I can. A byproduct is that I am able to return to work rested and refreshed for the work ahead."

Spiritual rest encourages enjoyment of God, others, and God's creation.

▶ If you could really unplug and enjoy the Sabbath rest the article describes, what activity(ies) could you pursue to celebrate God, people, and creation instead of the ways you're tempted to pursue work or leisure apart from God?

LEADER'S NOTES

LEADER'S NOTE: Read this introduction as a group or ask group members to read it before or after your first meeting. Whenever you read it, be sure to impress on everyone that they have a "calling" or vocation.

HOW TO USE THIS STUDY

Each lesson is designed to take around 1–1 ½ hour(s) to complete. If your group has more time available, you can simply spend a little longer in the Discussion and Exercise sections. Each lesson will include the following elements:

Bible Conversation	Exercise
We want to start by talking about the Bible together. As the name suggests, this section is designed to stimulate your thinking and prepare you and your group for the ideas that will be presented in each lesson.	Each of the exercises in this study is designed to help you make practical applications of the concepts being taught, or help you understand the content at a deeper heart level. Be sure to allow enough time for your group to adequately work through and discuss the exercises as directed.
Article	**Wrap-Up**
The written articles are the primary source of the teaching content for each lesson. They are short, clear teachings of the concepts being presented in the lesson. Each week, your group will take a few minutes to read the article out loud together.	The wrap-up gives the leader the chance to answer any last minute questions, reinforce ideas, and most importantly spend a few minutes praying as a group.
Discussion	
This section is where we communally process the concepts being taught in the article. Often the discussion will work in conjunction with the next section (exercise) to help flesh out the teaching and apply it to our lives in concrete ways.	

lesson

THE GOSPEL-CENTERED LIFE:
GOD REALIGNS US TO WORK

BIG IDEA

For many of us, work is just a set of things we must do—jobs and activities that can be stressful, unfulfilling, and demanding, and that seem to have little to do with God. For others, work is what defines and gives personal value or significance. But God has something better in mind for his children than either of these options. A gospel-centered understanding of work—which puts Christ and what he has done for us at the center of all we do—transforms work from a set of things we do for survival or validation to become our *vocation*, a calling from Jesus to love, serve, and follow him. This makes work one of the primary ways we respond to God in gratitude for all he has done for us in Christ. It's also a primary way we participate with God's people to bring healing, hope, and gospel witness to a broken world.

LESSON OVERVIEW

I. Bible Conversation	Read and talk about the passage(s) [10-20 min]
II. Article	*A Deeper Understanding of Vocation* [10 min]
III. Discussion	Process *A Deeper Understanding of Vocation* together [15-20 min]
IV. Exercise	*Extraordinary Purposes in Ordinary Work* [15-25 min]
V. Wrap-Up	Final thoughts and prayer [5-10 min]

BIBLE CONVERSATION *10-20 minutes*

We are focusing on three big questions in this lesson.

1. What is our functional set of beliefs (not the spiritual "right" answer, but what we really think) as we approach work and daily life?

2. What were work and life designed by God to look like?

3. How does the gospel speak into the gap between these two realities (1 and 2)?

The questions and Bible passages we explore will highlight the differences between our actual beliefs and what God intends.

They also point to our need for the Holy Spirit to

- continually refocus us on God as we go about our work,

- fill us with faith to trust and depend on him, and

- grow us in our love for God and others as we go about our daily callings.

SET-UP It can be hard to see our life as a seamless, interwoven fabric that integrates our personal faith with the work God has called us to do. Given society's distrust of faith in the marketplace and our own brokenness, we are tempted to keep faith and work separate. We may want to live for Christ in everything we do, but our faith often winds up being confined to the private sphere of life. Our work doesn't reflect the fact that it is something God has prepared for us to do. Instead it simply comes to reflect our own goals, desires, and methods for getting what we want. We don't even know how to ask how faith in Christ connects with what we're doing.

When this happens, work takes on a role in our lives it was never intended to have. For some, work comes to feel like a burden, something we simply "have to do" in order to survive. For others, it becomes the center of our lives, a false but powerful source of identity. But neither option reflects a gospel-centered understanding of work, which acknowledges that our work was distorted by the fall but has been made new in Christ as a way to live out our calling from God.

If our perspective on work is mostly about just surviving, we will look to leisure as a deliverance from the daily grind ("I'm working for the weekend. I just can't wait until I'm retired.") If we see work as the center and focus of life that gives meaning, purpose, and gratification, we'll be too busy to do anything else. ("I'll spend time with my family and church when I finish this project. What I do *is* who I am.") This first lesson digs deeper into assumptions like these that minimize our calling from Jesus and their impact on our work lives. We will also consider what it means to be called into partnership with God in our daily life.

ASK What excites you or brings you joy about what you do at work/school/home?

ASK What things drive you crazy about life at work/school/home? Why do you do what you do at work/school/home?

ASK Would you take on your current role (worker/student/caregiver) if you didn't have to? If you didn't need a paycheck to make ends meet, what would you do?

Next, let's look at some Bible passages that deal with the good and bad in our work.

READ The first passages we want to look at are Genesis 1:26—2:2, Genesis 2:15, and Genesis 3:17–24.

ASK What do these passages say about God's relationship to us? What do these passages say about how we respond to God?

LEADER'S NOTE: We're primarily looking for answers about the kinds of work God is engaged in here. God's work reflects his character. He creates by making something out of nothing. He sustains all he has made. He comes to redeem what has been broken. We also see that we've been created to bear his image and called to reflect his character. He models both work and rest for us as created beings who enjoy relationship with him, imitate him, and learn from him. Life before our fall into sin was simple, good, and relational. God created a garden for our provision and enjoyment, to give us legitimate, dignifying work in partnership with him while we met our physical needs. God also provided us with boundaries (rest and the Tree of Knowledge of Good and Evil) for our work.

The passage that deals with the fall tells us that even after we sin, God provides for us. We see that we tend to ignore God's boundaries and warnings and often avoid repentance without God's prodding. Finally, we see that even in the midst of toil, sweat, and pain in our work today, we have God's imprint on us in our underlying desire for relationship with our Creator and for purpose and meaning in our work.

READ The final passage we want to look at in this lesson is Romans 8:11–22.

ASK What does this passage say about God's relationship to us? What does this passage say about how we respond to God?

LEADER'S NOTE: When we trust in Christ to forgive our sins and bring us into God's family, all things become new, starting with the spiritual life he gives us and the presence and power of the Holy Spirit within us. We respond to God by giving him our whole lives in love and service. God adopts us and we respond by calling him "Abba Father." God makes us heirs; we respond by sharing in the sufferings of Jesus. God is glorifying us alongside Jesus. We look forward to our ultimate glorification because it represents our freedom and a return to the way life was meant to be. In fact, the whole creation eagerly awaits the renewal and restoration God will someday complete.

TRANSITION TO ARTICLE: These passages give us a biblical understanding of God's calling to follow him in all spheres of life, including the work he gives us. God's design is for men and women to know themselves as partners in his continuing work in the world. Through our work and by his power, even now God is redeeming, sustaining, and re-creating all things. To get a fuller understanding of this reality, let's read an article together and then go through some discussion questions.

ARTICLE *10 minutes*

TURN TO ARTICLE: *A Deeper Understanding of Vocation*

Read aloud, taking turns at the breaks between paragraphs.

LEADER'S NOTE: We're not looking for terribly profound answers to the following questions. Instead we want the group to draw one or two meaningful ideas from this lesson. Hopefully this will move group members from cynicism about the fallenness and drudgery of work to recognition that work is a gift from God with the potential to be used for good.

DISCUSSION *15-20 minutes*

Let's think about some of the main ideas from the article.

ASK What ideas from the article resonated with you?

ASK How does a gospel perspective drive this new way of viewing work?

ASK How does a gospel perspective correct and challenge some of the misguided ways we might have come to understand our work?

Let's make these ideas a little more personal.

ASK How might making Jesus the functional center of your life change the way you view your work?

EXERCISE *15-25 minutes*

We've begun exploring our need to exchange misguided views of work for ones better aligned with God's Word, Jesus's work on our behalf, and his purposes for us. ***Extraordinary Purposes in Ordinary Work*** helps us see simple ways we participate in God's work that may be obscured by our cultural assumptions. In this exercise, you'll see how your everyday work parallels God's work of creation, provision, and redemption in the world.

TURN TO the ***Extraordinary Purposes in Ordinary Work*** exercise. If there is time, read through the exercise and have the group brainstorm some ideas to get started.

You can also assign these exercises for homework if you're running out of time.

WRAP-UP *5-10 minutes*

Take questions, comments, and lead group in prayer.

lesson

2 TRANSFORMATION:
GOD USES WORK TO CHANGE US

BIG IDEA

Work was created to be a good thing, but after the fall it became one of the main areas where our sin and brokenness show up. However, our workplaces are not beyond God's care and purpose. He is more than able to use the fallen things in life to grow us to be more like Christ. If we keep the truths of the gospel in mind as we pursue our work, it elevates work from a daily grind to the space where God is at work in us to deepen our relationship to him, to one another, and to creation as we partner with him in his plans and purposes.

LESSON OVERVIEW

I. Bible Conversation   Read and talk about the passage(s) [10-20 min]

II. Article   *The Daily Grind* [10 min]

III. Discussion   Process concepts of *The Daily Grind* together [15-20 min]

IV. Exercise   *How Work Reveals Our Hearts* [15-25 min]

V. Wrap-Up   Final thoughts and prayer [5-10 min]

BIBLE CONVERSATION *10-20 minutes*

Since we spend so much time working (at school, marketplace, home, etc.), the workplace is the primary setting for our vocational partnership with God. And simultaneously it's also potentially one of the most significant places for our personal transformation into the likeness of Christ. Neither one happens if we keep our work separate from the promises and purposes we discover in the gospel. Instead, work can become a burden that is empty of meaning—or take over our lives as a great, but false, source of value. As an alternative, we can understand work from a gospel perspective and allow it to draw us to rely on Christ in greater ways.

SET-UP At breakfast one morning my friend Charlie confided in me, "My work is awful. I just want to quit because. . . ." Maybe you know how you would finish Charlie's statement. As we discussed last time, work was designed as part of God's good creation and as a way for us to partner with God in the stewardship of his world. Like every other aspect of our lives, sin has twisted our relationship toward work so that it has the dual capacity to be filled with toil and trouble as well as joy and beauty. Too often our temptation is to retreat and look for ways to protect ourselves from potential trouble and temptation. Although this is a natural response, it can short-circuit the plans God may have for us. He is always encouraging us to rely on him more deeply by faith, even in the midst of trials, temptations, and suffering. He wants us to call out to him in our distress so that he can meet us and spiritually transform us and our workplaces in the hard times.

First, consider Charlie's comment: "My work is awful. I just want to quit because. . . ."

ASK If you were saying that to a trusted friend, how would you end that sentence?

Let's consider a gospel perspective on suffering and persevering in times of trial.

ASK Why might Paul be particularly qualified to talk about God's care in times of trial and testing? What parts of Paul's story help us understand his qualifications?

LEADER'S NOTE: Paul underwent trial and imprisonment for his faith in Christ. He spoke of his thorn in the flesh and his record of religious achievement before meeting Christ. He knew what it is to suffer and what it is to be delivered.

Let's see what Paul says to the churches in Rome and Corinth about this topic.

The first is a passage we looked at in the last lesson, but one that is useful here as well.

`READ` Romans 8:18–21

`READ` 1 Corinthians 10:13

`ASK` What benefits does Paul suggest come through suffering and testing?

`ASK` How is God present with us during these times?

LEADER'S NOTE: Because times of trial and testing in life are universal, you can count on group members to refer to times of personal trial. Affirm any ideas that align with Paul's thoughts in the passages but then encourage group members to consider the benefits Paul lists in Romans 8 and 1 Corinthians 10. Here are some:
1. *Suffering increases our longing for creation to be released from bondage and our desire for greater freedom from sin as God's children.*
2. *Temptations offer us a chance to see God's faithfulness in our time of need.*
3. *Resisting temptation strengthens our reliance on God as our deliverer in times of trial.*

Now let's consider what James says about the importance of both our beliefs and actions in times of trial and temptation.

READ James 1:2–12

ASK What are three things James says about the value of trials and temptations?

LEADERS NOTE: James talks about three similar things. Trials are a form of testing that produce:

1. *Steadfastness in faith*
2. *Completeness or wholeness and unity with Christ/Crown of Life*
3. *Wisdom that comes through experience*

Finally, consider your own testing and refining.

ASK How have you found these principles to be relevant in your own life?

TRANSITION TO ARTICLE: We want to think more deeply about personal hardships as we read about the suffering present in daily life. Try to think of ways the personal experiences of trial, temptation, toil, and suffering might relate to the categories developed in **The Daily Grind** article we'll read together.

ARTICLE *10 minutes*

TURN TO: *The Daily Grind* article in your Participants Guide. Read aloud, taking turns at paragraph breaks.

DISCUSSION *15-20 minutes*

LEADER'S NOTE: Like last time, profound answers aren't critical here. We want folks to track with the article and take one or two nuggets of truth home with them, especially as it relates to God's purposes being worked out in times of trouble. God's love for us is never thwarted by sin. He is always caring and providing for us, even in times of temptation or trial. For this reason we can resist and grieve suffering as hardship but also accept it because it has been sifted through God's hands to help us rely more deeply by faith on his strength.

Let's think about some of the main ideas from the article.

ASK What are some of your initial thoughts about this article?

ASK Do you believe God puts us in situations of toil, trial, and testing?

Let's make these ideas a little more personal.

ASK Where has God placed you in situations of toil, trial, or testing?

ASK Are you a person who is more likely to resist or to accept hardship in your life?

ASK Why might both resisting AND accepting hardship be important responses for us as people who proclaim Christ to others?

EXERCISE *15-25 minutes*

We're exploring how God uses situations to transform our character by aligning us with his character and purposes *and* exposing our sinful motivations. *How Work Reveals Our Hearts* helps us identify ways that our perspective on work might be clouded by wrong, self-centered motivations rather than a Christ-centered perspective.

TURN TO: *How Work Reveals Our Hearts.* Review the activity with the group and encourage participants to work on the exercise this coming week.

WRAP-UP *5-10 minutes*

Take questions, comments, and lead group in prayer.

FROM TOIL TO FAITH:

DESIRING A NEW WAY TO LIVE

BIG IDEA

This lesson helps us identify patterns in the ways we fail to integrate our faith with our work. These patterns often point to the deep idols that undermine the way we relate to our heavenly Father and our neighbors as well. First, we'll see how our "functional idols" might be affecting our behavior; then we'll consider the ways we need to repent and welcome the work of the Holy Spirit in our lives (2 Corinthians 5:17).

Our status as God's children compels us to put off sin and to put on a new way of living by faith—to shed old ways of relating and to welcome new gospel-centered ones instead (Ephesians 4 and Colossians 3). A gospel-centered understanding of work leads us to repent of "bent" coping patterns and deep idols and to more fully participate in God's work in the world as we are conformed to the likeness of Jesus.

LESSON OVERVIEW

I. Bible Conversation	Read and talk about the passage(s) [10-20 min]	
II. Article	***Our Flawed Methods*** [10 min]	
III. Discussion	Think through some personal implications of a Christ-centered perspective and imagine new ways of relating to those around you [15-20 min]	

IV. Exercise	***Pretending and Performing at Work*** [15–25 min]
V. Wrap-Up	Final thoughts and prayer [5–10 min]

BIBLE CONVERSATION *10-20 minutes*

Understanding all that Jesus has accomplished for us enables us to see our daily lives as a partnership with God in his work in the world. He wants our lives to reflect his passionate heart for a restored creation and redeemed humanity. God also desires that we do all we do to his glory and honor. We've looked at how God uses the hard things in our work to make us more like Jesus and how those tests and trials can lead us to repent and turn from the deeper idols that have motivated us. In this lesson we'll talk about how and why we often give in to functional idols that hinder the power of Christ in our work. We call the patterns that minimize the gospel's impact on our lives *pretending* and *performing*. Resisting God's work in our lives always involves one of these two patterns. *Pretense* minimizes sin by making ourselves out to be something we are not, and *performance* reduces God's standards to something we can meet.

SET-UP Each of the following parables involves people who experienced God's love and provision but failed to *put off* false ways of relating and *put on* truth. They chose to be controlled by their appetites and the pressures of life rather than live in light of the truth they had experienced from God. These stories may seem familiar to you. As you read them, put yourself in the position of the main character who is failing to grasp the truth.

READ The first parable is the story of the unmerciful servant, one of a number of stories Jesus told when a Zealot asked him who would be the greatest in the kingdom of heaven. Would someone read Matthew 18:21–35 aloud?

ASK How did the servant fail in his response? What should his response have been?

ASK Can you remember a time when you failed to be merciful, forgiving, and generous despite the fact that God has been merciful, forgiving, and generous to you? Have you held others to standards in the workplace (or elsewhere) that you can't meet yourself? What does that reveal about your reliance on the gospel's power in your life?

READ Our second story is about the lost sons, told in response to the Pharisees' complaint that Jesus was hanging out with sinners and tax collectors. One son clings to his own righteousness, and one begs for forgiveness. In this reading put yourself in the place of the brother who does everything right but resents his father's generosity toward his sibling. Will someone read Luke 15:11–32 for us?

ASK You may work or live alongside people who think like the older brother. They do not live in light of the Father's love for them but live in the light of their own rightness, viewing themselves falsely and dispensing justice when mercy is required. Such people may justify and build themselves up but miss the bigger picture of how much they've been loved and forgiven. Some may become overtly dishonest; others are more subtle. How do you relate to them?

ASK How does the Father relate to the older brother?

ASK How does the story of the two brothers and generous father speak to your own struggles of missing the gospel with performance and pretense and with being proud of your performance more than you are grateful for God's mercy?

TRANSITION TO ARTICLE: Every context we move into has its own set of values and expectations. As we move from context to context and encounter those new expectations, they can easily overwhelm us so that we forget our partnership in the kingdom of God and God's call on our lives. The way out of this forgetfulness is repentance that flows from knowledge of the righteousness of Christ and knowledge that we are beloved children of our heavenly Father. As we remember whose we are, we also need to understand what we are repenting from and what we are being conformed to. In *Our Flawed Methods* we'll examine a few of the approaches that "religious" people often take as they relate to the context of their daily life and work. Then we'll discuss an alternative gospel approach.

ARTICLE *10 minutes*

`TURN TO ARTICLE` *Our Flawed Methods*

DISCUSSION *15-20 minutes*

LEADER'S NOTE: It might be hard for group members to come up with examples if this is their first time hearing about performance and pretense. Don't push it if this exercise seems too abstract for some. The goal is simply to help the group recognize the underlying pitfalls of pretense and performance and how these might surface in their own work situations.

`ASK` Where have you seen these flawed approaches of pretense and performance?

`ASK` How is accepting these "old" ways dangerous for us?

`ASK` How are you tempted to succumb to this thinking in your work, home, or school?

`ASK` What would it look like to be a gospel presence in your current environment?

`ASK` What are some old ways you need to put off or new ways you can put on?

EXERCISE *15-25 minutes*

How do we miss opportunities for gospel transformation in our own lives? Are we blind to the influences around us that sway us from the gospel? To gain a better understanding of the way we're impacted by performance and pretense here's an exercise to help decode the patterns of your daily life.

`TURN TO:` *Pretending and Performing at Work*

WRAP-UP *5-10 minutes*

Ask God to open your eyes to his work and presence this week.

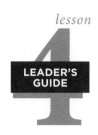
IMAGE-BEARERS:
A GOSPEL LOOK AT THE IMAGE OF GOD

BIG IDEA

When our eyes are opened to God's work, we participate in it just by seeing the world from a gospel perspective—being observant wherever he has placed us, ready to speak and act according to what we've come to know through faith in Jesus. Our adoption into God's household as well-loved children qualifies us to walk in partnership with him. Our work—though we are tugged in so many different directions by people and institutions that want to conform us into *their* image—is nevertheless being transformed by God through our faithful gospel presence. It is no accident that God has placed you where you are. Through your presence, you reflect God's character as one of his *Image-Bearers* to those around you.

LESSON OVERVIEW

I. Bible Conversation   Read and talk about the passage(s) [10–20 min]

II. Article   *Image-Bearers in God's Economy* [10 min]

III. Discussion   Process concepts of *Image-Bearers in God's Economy* [15–20 min]

IV. Exercise   *Ordinary Work, Extraordinary Opportunity* [15–25 min]

V. Wrap-Up   Final thoughts and prayer [5–10 min]

BIBLE CONVERSATION *10-20 minutes*

The gospel transforms our perspective on work. Instead of it being an idolatrous temptation or source of toil, pain, and frustration, work becomes a way to reflect God's image in daily life. When we trust in Christ, we soon see that God has been going before us to encourage and guide us as his children. By faith our hearts turn from fear to worship as we reflect his image and glorify him wherever he has placed us. The promises and power of the gospel free us to reveal God's imprint on our lives as we faithfully serve where he has called us.

SET-UP Because of Jesus's work in our lives, image-bearers are freed from a fear of circumstances and have new eyes to see God's work. A daily relationship of repentance and faith with our Creator, empowered by knowing that in Christ we have received his perfect life and are accepted and loved by our heavenly Father, is the foundation for a renewed perspective on our work.

In 2 Corinthians 4:4 we are told that Satan has blinded the world in sin, leaving unbelievers cut off from the things of God. Spiritual blindness comes with and from idolatry and a preoccupation with the things of this world. The unspiritual worry and say, "What shall we eat?" "What shall we drink?" "What shall we wear?" (Matthew 6:31). Their mental energy and physical strength are absorbed in their present circumstances rather than the things of God in gratitude for his provision.

In today's Bible Conversation we will look at two passages that show how God's power can free us to see our circumstances with eyes of faith and thus better reflect the restored image of God. We'll look at one Old Testament passage and one New Testament passage. These passages may be familiar, but consider what they teach us about being witnesses to God's work in history.

READ The first story is about Elisha and his servant, who are surrounded by the Syrian army that stands ready to destroy them. Would someone read 2 Kings 6:8–23 aloud?

LEADERS NOTE: This can be a confusing story because the prophet Elisha is not directly named. The "Man of God" referenced here is Elisha.

ASK What is happening here?

Why do you think Elisha's servant could not see Israel's chariots at first?

What enabled Elisha's servant to see the reality around him?

Why is it important that Elisha's servant (not just Elisha) gained a different perspective on that day?

How does faith grow in our lives?

LEADERS NOTE: There is a tremendous importance that Elisha's servant was able to see what Elisha saw so that it could be verified and given to us as Scripture. We need others in our lives to strengthen our faith and open our eyes to what God is doing, just like Elisha did for his servant. Sometimes we even need their prayers.

`ASK` Was there ever a time when you or someone you know lacked the faith for a godly perspective on life's circumstances?

What changed you or them as you/they struggled in this manner?

`READ` The second passage is Ephesians 1:15–23. These verses are one long, rich and profound sentence that spills out from Paul in worship and joy. Would someone read Ephesians 1:15–23 aloud?

`ASK` Why is Paul praying for the Ephesians this way? What is his motivation?

What are some things Paul is praying would happen in the Ephesians' lives?

Take a look at the phrase "having the eyes of your hearts enlightened."

Why is it important that the Ephesians' hearts (and ours) are enlightened? What is the alternative? What is the source and result of their enlightenment?

`ASK` How do these passages relate to being image-bearers where God places us?

`TRANSITION TO ARTICLE` When Jesus is our Savior and the center of our lives, he changes us at a foundational level, giving us a new perspective on our life and work. Knowing God and trusting him gives us eyes of faith to see beyond our circumstances to the work God is doing all around us. God has enlisted us, as members of his family, to share in the responsibilities and opportunities of his kingdom rule. He is including us in something much bigger and more beautiful than anything we might have imagined. Let's turn to an article that looks at the surprising characteristics of image-bearers in God's kingdom household.

ARTICLE *10 minutes*

`TURN TO` the article *Image-Bearers in God's Economy* and read it aloud, taking turns at paragraph breaks.

DISCUSSION *15-20 minutes*

Let's think about some of the main ideas from the article.

`ASK` What ideas from this article are new or interesting to you?

`ASK` How might these ideas change your outlook on your own work or free you up to work differently?

EXERCISE *15-25 minutes*

We've been talking about motivations for work. Help diagnose your perspectives and motivations by working through a personal case study in **Ordinary Work, Extraordinary Opportunity.**

`TURN TO:` **Ordinary Work, Extraordinary Opportunity.** If there is time, review the exercise or assign it as homework.

WRAP-UP *5-10 minutes*

Take questions, comments, and lead group in prayer.

A NEW ATTITUDE:
IMITATING GOD IN A WORLD OF WORK

BIG IDEA

As we saw in the last lesson, God gives men and women talents that can be used to reflect his image and character. Ultimately we offer ourselves to God's service to help bring the blessings of his kingdom into this world. The gospel makes us loved sons and daughters and changes our work from something we do for personal gain to something we do as *Imitators of God* who are eager to carry out his will.

LESSON OVERVIEW

I. Bible Conversation	Read and talk about the passage(s) [10-20 min]	
II. Article	***Extreme Work: Striving and Sloth*** [10 min]	
III. Discussion	Process concepts of ***Extreme Work*** article [15-20 min]	
IV. Exercise	***Life Integration Diagnostic*** [15-25 min]	
V. Wrap-Up	Final thoughts and prayer [5-10 min]	

BIBLE CONVERSATION *10-20 minutes*

Too many of us use human standards of success and failure to measure the value of our work instead of considering how our work is making us more like Jesus. We may not realize it, but we have abused the relationships, situations, and roles God has given us whenever we have used them to pursue own idolatrous goals rather than seeking to imitate God in his work. Is it because we think we have earned our roles and relationships rather than having them entrusted to us by God? Are we ignorant of how a gospel perspective helps us to pursue our work in faith? Christ's work on our behalf should keep us from being fixated on ourselves. When we identify with Jesus, we're freed up to be imitators of our creative, sustaining, and redeeming heavenly Father.

SET-UP Who we are should shape what we do. As image-bearers who reflect God and share in his work, we are not in our circumstances by chance. God is using us as his partners in the roles and opportunities entrusted to us. It brings him joy for us to bear his image and imitate his work. Jesus's work in our lives frees up time and effort we once spent responding to circumstances in fear and shame. His Spirit allows love to flow to others through our work.

As our salvation and new identity in Christ are worked out in our lives, we begin to see where we have God-given influence in our home and workplace. This gives us courage to step into those places of influence as imitators of God. We come to see that we were made to shape those contexts for God's glory and the advance of the gospel.

Let's look at some passages that get below the surface of our lives to deal with our motivations. In the first passage, Moses is commissioning Israel as they are about to enter the Promised Land. Though he is left behind because of his own disobedience, he reminds them of God's law and of who God is.

READ Deuteronomy 4:1–9

ASK What does Moses propose as the motivation for listening to God and doing what he commands (imitating God)?

LEADER'S NOTE: The critical answer here is that receiving the land as an inheritance reflects Israel's position as God's beloved children. The coming kingdom of God is their destiny. So the most important thing for them and us is to "cling" or "hold fast" to the Lord as the only hope against idols that lead to destruction. The land is not their hope—God is.

ASK What are some sub-benefits listed here? Why are they important?

LEADER'S NOTE: The nations are watching what is happening (v. 6, "in the sight of the peoples"). What will amaze them is how near God is as he dwells among his people rather than far off. (He appears to his people as a pillar of smoke and cloud of fire.) Likewise their keeping of the law and imitating God will bring wisdom and understanding to all the nations.

Now, let's look at Christ's work on our behalf.

READ Hebrews 2:9–11 and 14–18

ASK What is Christ's understanding of our individual circumstances?

ASK What are some implications of willingly walking into situations of suffering and trouble as people who follow and imitate Jesus?

LEADER'S NOTE: Jesus sees and honors us. He empowers our obedience and takes on our failure so we can be free from guilt and shame, free to act as his beloved brothers and sisters.

READ Galatians 2:20–21

ASK What do these verses say about how we should be motivated in daily life?

ASK What do you think it means for us to frustrate or nullify the grace of God?

ASK How might your lifestyle be nullifying God's grace?

`ASK` How is the motivation of Galatians 2 similar to the Israelites "holding fast" or "clinging to the Lord" in Deuteronomy 4?

`TRANSITION TO ARTICLE:` Our imitation of God's work can deviate toward two extremes: striving and sloth. At first these stances appear to be opposites, but when we examine their underlying causes, they become surprisingly equivalent.

When work is our master (when we're enslaved to our work and *strive* toward it as our ultimate goal rather than being willing imitators of God), we have exalted work to be an idol in our lives (something we value and "worship" more than God). When work is seen as drudgery to avoid because we're bent toward laziness or leisure, we suffer from an opposite form of idolatry. Under the sway of *sloth*, the desire to "strike it rich" by manipulating the system or to "just get by" with minimal effort can be appealing. But again, there is no desire to imitate God in how and why we work. The extent to which we look to work as our salvation or our misery shows how career or leisure have become functional idols or masters.

Both extremes stem from misunderstanding the nature of work as something given by God for our good and his glory. As you read ***Extreme Work***, consider how you might be affected.

ARTICLE *10 minutes*

`TURN TO` the article ***Extreme Work: Striving and Sloth*** and read it aloud, taking turns at paragraph breaks.

DISCUSSION *15-20 minutes*

Let's think about some of the main ideas from the article.

`ASK` How are striving and sloth similar?

`ASK` How does a hub-oriented or gospel-centered approach correct the ways we pursue our labor and its fruits?

`ASK` How do striving and sloth shrink the work of the cross? (Think about ways they can represent both pretending and performing.)

Let's make these ideas a little more personal.

`ASK` Do you need to repent of any motivations you have toward your work?

EXERCISE *15–25 minutes*

In **Extreme Work: Striving and Sloth** we've been talking about motivations for work. Help diagnose your motivations with a personal case study in **Life Integration Diagnostic.**

`TURN TO:` **Life Integration Diagnostic.** If there is time, review the exercise with the group or assign it for homework.

WRAP-UP *5–10 minutes*

Take questions, comments, and lead group in prayer.

BOND-SERVANTS:
FROM SLAVES TO SONS AND DAUGHTERS

BIG IDEA

Some of us have been freed from a love of money, others from self-righteousness or self-importance, and others from self-hatred. We are all new people who owe our lives to Jesus. As we grow in our understanding of the gospel, we grow in gratitude and want to follow and worship the One who has given us new life! God doesn't treat us as workers, valued only for what we do, but as his sons and daughters, loved for who we are in Christ. What we do never defines who we are; our relationship to Jesus matters far more. Rather than our work being our identity, Jesus offers us true personhood as trusted sons and daughters in God's family.

LESSON OVERVIEW

I. Bible Conversation	Read and talk about the passage(s) [10–20 min]
II. Article	***The Freedom of Serving God in Our Work*** [10 min]
III. Discussion	Process ***The Freedom of Serving God in Our Work*** [15–20 min]
IV. Exercise	***From Work Expectations to Love Commands*** [15–25 min]
V. Wrap-Up	Final thoughts and prayer [5–10 min]

BIBLE CONVERSATION *10-20 minutes*

Throughout the New Testament, Christ's followers refer to themselves *as Bond-servants*— those who live under Christ's authority and desire to serve and represent him in all they do. Just as we do in marriage, bond-servants choose voluntarily to integrate their identity with the identity of someone else, for better or worse. Peter calls himself a bond-servant of Jesus Christ in 2 Peter 1:1; Paul says the same in Romans 1:1, James in James 1:1, Jude in Jude 1, and finally John in Revelation 1:1.[1] These men all start their letters with a declaration of their bond-service to Jesus, which should make us wonder what the idea meant to them and how it can impact us.

SET-UP Christ's bond-servants serve him not because they must, but because it is their desire. In ancient times, bond-servants were people who were trapped in circumstances that cost them their freedom. Because they were in debt, they had to sell themselves to a master for a period of time and use the money to pay off what they owed. They then served their master until they had worked off their debt to him. But sometimes the servant did not want to be set free; he preferred to continue serving his master, making the arrangement permanent.

Those who had been mistreated would not choose to become bond-servants, however those who could say, "I love my master . . . I will not go out free" (Exodus 21:5), could stay on to work as servants out of gratitude and trust. Like them, believers belong to Christ, who paid the debt of our sin and freed us from spiritual bondage. We owe our lives and freedom to Christ, and we choose to serve him as bond-servants forever. We know there is no better life apart from Christ. As bond-servants, our work contributes to his work of bringing redemption and liberation to this world.

Let's look at two passages that deal with moving from slavery to freedom in Christ. We'll start with the parable of the talents. This might seem like

---

1. Note: Modern translations like NIV and ESV translate *doulos* as **servant** throughout for fear of misunderstanding and negative associations with the term "bond-servant." "Bond-servant" is a more precise translation of the original text, which we'll delve into more deeply in this lesson.

an odd place to start, but we want to examine it as a negative example, to think about the motivations of the unfaithful servant.

READ Matthew 25:14–30. Keep in mind that a talent was roughly equivalent to a lifetime's wages for an average worker.

ASK Is there a reason given why the servants were entrusted with different quantities?

ASK In a gospel context, what kind of ability (v. 15) do you think God uses to measure us?

LEADER'S NOTE: Don't spend a lot of time trying to define ability or talent here. There are two important things to note from the passage as it relates to the two questions. (1) The master does not treat his servants equally, and (2) those who were praised for their ability to invest their resources were told, "Well done, good and faithful servant." Their ability or talent seems correlated to their capacity or cap-ability to serve the master faithfully in the tasks given them. The master doesn't expect their faithfulness to exceed the resources he has given them.

ASK What is the stated reason that the last servant hid his talents rather than investing what he had been given to develop the master's interests?

ASK Do you think the last servant knew and understood the master?

(Hint: Was he grateful for what he'd been given, and did he risk it?)

Now let's turn to one of the apostle Paul's statements on his status as a bond-servant and its relation to the gospel.

READ Galatians 1:9–12

ASK What does Paul seek as a bond-servant? What doesn't he seek?

ASK What is Paul's attitude toward those who proclaim the need to serve God out of fear to try to earn his approval? What is his attitude toward those who please men out of fear in an attempt to win their approval? How are the two related?

LEADER'S NOTE: Those who serve out of a fear of man or who try to earn God's approval are putting themselves under a curse. Both are impossible tasks that lead to destruction rather than salvation. The only real path Paul sees is serving Christ in gratitude for what he's done.

`ASK` What is Paul's stated attitude in all he does?

`TRANSITION TO ARTICLE:` We want to think more deeply about the implications of serving Christ in gratitude by reading *The Freedom of Serving God in Our Work.*

ARTICLE *10 minutes*

`TURN TO` the article *The Freedom of Serving God in Our Work* and read it aloud, taking turns at paragraph breaks.

DISCUSSION *15-20 minutes*

Let's think about some of the main ideas from the article.

`ASK` How is gratitude for God's generosity different as a motivation from personal guilt or a desire to earn a righteous position before God?

`ASK` Has the Holy Spirit ever prompted you to do more than the minimum with a coworker, client or peer, when the minimum was what was expected? What did that extravagant action look like?

`ASK` How might God be prompting you to consider going above and beyond what is required of you in a relationship or circumstance?

EXERCISE *15-25 minutes*

In *The Freedom of Serving God in Our Work* we've been talking about motivations for work. Help diagnose your motivations by working through your personal reflections in *From Work Expectations to Love Commands*.

TURN TO: *From Work Expectations to Love Commands.* If there is time, review the exercise with the group. Otherwise, assign for homework.

WRAP-UP *5-10 minutes*

Take questions, comments, and lead group in prayer.

lesson

LEADER'S GUIDE

7 STEWARDS:
SERVING JESUS BY SERVING OTHERS

BIG IDEA

Every opportunity that enters our lives is given by God. He wants us to represent him in ways that bring him glory and impact others with good works and the gospel. The Greek word for *Steward* is closely tied to the idea of being an agent—someone who is given resources and opportunities to carry out someone else's mission and purposes. Today, this idea lies behind the work of real estate agents, insurance agents, and secret agents. These modern stewards are equipped to act within a specific context to promote the interests of a known other.

We respond to the circumstances God gives us in ways that either conform to God's will or are opposed to it. God's provision for us as his children transforms our orphan attitudes about resources like time and money to uncover ways to seek the good of others with everything he has entrusted to us, in service to our Savior.

LESSON OVERVIEW

I. Bible Conversation	Read and talk about the passage(s) [10-20 min]
II. Article	***Two Aspects of Stewardship*** [10 min]
III. Discussion	Process concepts of ***Two Aspects of Stewardship*** [15-20 min]
IV. Exercise	***My Agenda, God's Agenda*** [15-25 min]
V. Wrap-Up	Final thoughts and prayer [5-10 min]

BIBLE CONVERSATION *10-20 minutes*

One underlying attitude of consumerism is to value people only for what they do or contribute to society. For all the benefits that come from a perspective of personal responsibility and freedom, such a system also creates a world of pride and shame in our workplaces, homes, neighborhoods, and schools. It exerts a tremendous pressure to perform because we're rewarded according to our next success or failure. Participants in such a system cut corners to win at all costs and use others for personal advantage. When we rely on our accomplishments instead of Christ, we worship ourselves and rarely share credit, overcome jealousy, or put the needs of others ahead of our own. Believers who live this way are buying into a form of self-righteousness to their peril. Such a motivational system can completely cut us off from the biblical reality of who we are as created persons with eternal souls.

SET-UP Our identity as God's beloved children means that we are to look to him for our provision, trust him with our future, and ask him to guide our daily actions. Being identified as God's beloved frees us to put the needs of others before our own and to celebrate their strengths and accomplishments because we know we will always be taken care of by our heavenly Father. Who we are is tied to Christ's righteousness and provision rather than our own merit or personal performance. Gratitude for God's love and Christ's work on our behalf is the motivating force for our work.

Let's look at two passages that consider the idea of being a servant in the kingdom of God, one from Jesus and one from Paul. The first highlights a teaching from Jesus that follows a discussion on who should be the greatest leader in the coming kingdom.

READ John 12:23–28

LEADER'S NOTE: The critical thing to note in this John 12 passage is that we need to die to ourselves and embrace the mission of Jesus to truly be fruitful in this world.

`ASK` Jesus starts his teaching on glory and servanthood by saying that a seed needs to die to be fruitful. What does this have to do with serving and glory?

`ASK` Jesus says that his Father will honor the one who serves him. What do you think that means for us as believers? What kind of honor is Jesus talking about?

`ASK` Jesus says he has a choice between being saved from this hour and glorifying the name of the Father. Why are these opposites for him?

`ASK` How is this concept true for us as we serve others in ways that glorify God?

`READ` 1 Corinthians 3:4–11

LEADER'S NOTE: Don't get wrapped up in Paul's and Apollos's roles here. Paul is explaining that their work was built on Christ's work, and that is what ultimately makes the difference. We all work alongside God and do not need to compete with one another for credit or for the fields in which we labor.

`ASK` What does it mean that "neither he who plants nor he who waters is anything"?

`ASK` Similarly, what does it mean that "he who plants and he who waters are one"?

`ASK` How are we all God's fellow workers?

`ASK` How is the work of Jesus our foundation?

`TRANSITION TO ARTICLE` In Mark 7:31 Jesus returns to Decapolis where he previously had cast out evil spirits from a possessed man and sent them into a herd of pigs, which then plunged over a cliff. Jesus urged the healed man to return to his household. This time Jesus was warmly welcomed (compared to the first time, when he was run off by an angry mob). We don't know what happened between the two visits, but we can assume that the demoniac—now visibly and radically changed to be in his right mind, restored to a normal daily life—was one thing that probably made a difference. Instead of Jesus encouraging this man to leave the familiar to follow him, Jesus told him to stay and be transformed where he was.

In the next article, *Two Aspects of Stewardship*, we'll see how our gratitude for Christ's work is a necessary precursor to being used as servants who display his glory—stewards in the kingdom of God representing Christ and his work on our behalf.

ARTICLE *10 minutes*

`TURN TO` *Two Aspects of Stewardship* and read it aloud, taking turns at paragraph breaks.

DISCUSSION *15-20 minutes*

`ASK` How are the visible qualities of a transformed life a catalyst for God's glory?

`ASK` How is it true that we must be united to Christ as bond-servants before we can grow into the role of stewards in his kingdom?

`ASK` What are some ways that your daily life is "a chief laboratory of the gospel"?

`ASK` Do you agree that, as stewards, joy is only possible when we willingly submit to Jesus serving us with his grace? Why is this so hard for us?

EXERCISE *15-25 minutes*

We are often motivated to serve ourselves—rather than God—in the activities of our day. *My Agenda, God's Agenda* considers how our daily activities can connect to ways God may be serving us—or wanting to serve the world through us. Use this exercise to see how God might be using you and desiring to change you through your daily circumstances.

`TURN TO:` Turn to the exercise *My Agenda, God's Agenda*. Review with the group if there is time. Otherwise assign for homework.

WRAP-UP *5-10 minutes*

Take questions, comments, and lead group in prayer.

AMBASSADORS:
REPRESENTATIVES SENT BY GOD

BIG IDEA

We are people who were once separated from God; now we represent him as we go to others with the good news of Jesus. Because we've been loved so well, as we go, we put aside our own goals and embrace our calling to extend God's kingdom, resting in God's provision, authority, and power. When we view life and work through gospel lenses, we see our neighbors as God sees them—broken people who need Jesus as much as we do.

LESSON OVERVIEW

I. Bible Conversation	Read and talk about the passage(s) [10-20 min]
II. Article	***Becoming Ambassadors*** [10 min]
III. Discussion	Process concepts of ***Becoming Ambassadors*** [15-20 min]
IV. Exercise	***People of Peace and Hospitality*** [15-25 min]
V. Wrap-Up	Final thoughts and prayer [5-10 min]

BIBLE CONVERSATION *10-20 minutes*

As those who have trusted in Christ, God is changing us right where we are so we can bring him glory as his *Ambassadors*. He sends us into circumstances, places, and relationships where he wants to be made known. Second Corinthians 5 says that we are Christ's ambassadors and that

God makes his appeal to others through our words and actions. By our presence we seek to persuade those around us to be reconciled to God. We begin by being in relationship with them, and Jesus promises to show up in the midst of that relationship. The New Testament word translated "ambassador" is *presbeuomen*. This word, along with similar words like "elder" and "(de)legate," assumes that we are God's representatives, acting on behalf of God and his people rather than looking to our own interests.

SET-UP One of the blessings of life is the opportunity to play a part in reconciling people to God. God has entrusted us with opportunities for service and a message of reconciliation. To use both opportunities well, we need the gift of repentance to see our own need of the gospel each day. How does the way God has loved me affect my view of others' circumstances? How does God view those around me? What is their greatest need, and how can I love them as I've been loved?

Let's look at a few passages that describe our role as ambassadors. We'll consider how shedding our tendency toward competitiveness and judgment changes us into people of peace and hospitality. We'll look at Jesus sending out the seventy-two and then see what Paul says about living as reconcilers as he models ambassadorship in the marketplace at Corinth.

READ Luke 10:1–11

ASK What characterizes this sending of new disciples by Jesus? Why do you think he tells them not to take supplies for their journey?

ASK What two things does Jesus tell his disciples to say to those who welcomed them? How are these two things significant? *(See verses 5 and 9.)*

LEADER'S NOTE: Jesus wanted the disciples to rely on their heavenly Father in all things and to look for people who were open to the gospel and hospitable to strangers. As they got to know these men and women in their homes, these households of hospitality would provide a "home away from home" for future travels as the disciples journeyed with Jesus.

ASK Are the disciples held responsible for the responses they receive from those they meet? Why is this important?

LEADER'S NOTE: God only holds the disciples responsible for their own faithfulness, living in openness to God's provision in all circumstances.

We have seen how Jesus prepared his disciples for future journeys to different cities and towns throughout Judea. Now, let's see what Paul the tentmaker says about ambassadorship in the kingdom of God.

READ 2 Corinthians 5:14–21

ASK Is reconciliation an absence of conflict or something more? What reconciliation have we received?

LEADER'S NOTE: Reconciliation is not just the absence of conflict; it includes the presence of deep relationship and trust and more importantly the resolution of conflict. When we reconcile we restore something that previously existed but was broken.

ASK How does trusting in God qualify us to be gospel-centered reconcilers?

LEADER'S NOTE: The gospel has helped us die to ourselves so that we can live and speak for Christ. Just as we are no longer viewed with judgment, so we can view others with a gospel perspective of who they are in Christ.

ASK Verse 16 says that we no longer have a "fleshly" or earthly perspective on anyone. In what ways does this reality change how we interact with people?

LEADER'S NOTE: We need to help people embrace their new status in Christ and never treat them according to the flesh or allow them to be defined by their past. We need to welcome and not condemn those who desire the freedom of Christ over and above the curse of sin and death. We need to call others to participate in the new creation of which we're now a part.

`ASK` Verse 19 says that in Christ God is doing two things: (1) reconciling the world to himself and (2) entrusting us with the message of reconciliation. What is the "message of reconciliation" entrusted to us? *(See verse 21.)*

ARTICLE *10 minutes*

`TURN TO` the article ***Becoming Ambassadors*** and read it aloud, taking turns at paragraph breaks.

DISCUSSION *15-20 minutes*

`ASK` Why is it important to spend time cultivating relationships with both believers and unbelievers?

`ASK` Are there ways that comparing yourself with others (either competing with them or looking down on them) prevents you from real friendships and authentic living?

`ASK` What are some situations you encounter through the week where you might be tempted to be competitive and/or defensive?

`ASK` How might knowing God's acceptance help when you are tempted to judge or be competitive with others?

`ASK` What are some simple but significant ways to bless those you spend time with at work, home, or school? What specific actions could you undertake to build others up rather than compete with them or tear them down?

EXERCISE *15-25 minutes*

We are thinking about our motivations and resources for sharing our faith with the people God puts in our lives. *People of Peace and Hospitality* helps us assess the ways pride or shame can keep us from sharing our faith with others.

TURN TO: *People of Peace and Hospitality.* Review the exercise with the group if there is time. Otherwise assign for homework.

WRAP-UP *5-10 minutes*

Take questions, comments, and lead group in prayer.

lesson

LEADER'S GUIDE

9 MESSENGERS:
GOD EQUIPS US WITH THE GOSPEL

BIG IDEA

God has entrusted us with our relationships. He has enlisted us as his *Messengers* in a mission to share the gospel with and make disciples of our children, friends, neighbors, and coworkers. In the past he used others to free us from our rebellion and to disciple us in the faith. Now he invites us to do the same in partnership with his Spirit. So, rather than being consumed by our personal agendas, the Spirit helps us to see that our lives are full of opportunities to share the good news with those who do not know Christ.

LESSON OVERVIEW

I. Bible Conversation	Read and talk about the passage(s) [10-20 min]
II. Article	*A New Outlook on Neighbors* [10 min]
III. Discussion	Process *A New Outlook on Neighbors* article [15-20 min]
IV. Exercise	*A Lifestyle of Love* [15-25 min]
V. Wrap-Up	Final thoughts and prayer [5-10 min]

BIBLE CONVERSATION *10-20 minutes*

Sometimes when we see ourselves as novices (as a student, starting out in a new job, etc.) we feel as if we have little to offer those with greater experience. The Bible sees such circumstances very differently. Paul's words to Timothy can be applied to anyone who is lower on the institutional totem pole: "Don't let anyone look down on you because you are young" (1 Timothy 4:12 NIV). Youth and inexperience might change the approach you use, but we need to remember the calling God has given us. In Romans 15 Paul says that he is speaking boldly because of the grace given to him. Because of the grace given to us, we too can forget ourselves and speak confidently about the freedom and power for change found in Christ.

Which is a more powerful way to reach those around us: working through a formulaic presentation of truth while we appear to have it all together or allowing people to see our honest struggles in disappointing circumstances and our efforts to apply the gospel to that situation?

How about the opposite end of the spectrum? What happens when there is a victory for the work team, a promotion, or another event that should lead to joy, but instead you feel hollow and empty? Do you hide these emotions and thoughts or do you use those struggles to let others see God working in your life? God can use anything to open doors for deeper conversations if we allow him.

We should be people who sow the seeds of the gospel wherever we go. God will show us what soil is fertile and where to go deeper. He is the One who hardens and softens, nurtures, and sends sun and rain to allow growth. We serve as his partners and allow him to do his work. Best of all, we witness what he is doing and share in his joy when the lost are found.

SET-UP What does God ask of us as messengers of the gospel? First, we are to be a faithful presence that loves and serves. Who we are and what we do are critical components of our message. Part of this is being candid with people about what God is doing in us and how we see him at work in the world. We also do this by welcoming personal conversation and questions on our perspective. While many people we interact with may not go to church (and may never do so), they can listen to us and have deeper spiritual conversations with us. When they see the openness we have to what God is doing in our lives, they will grow to trust us professionally, relationally, and spiritually as God works in their hearts and minds.

In our Bible Conversation and Article, we'll look at how spiritual conversations can naturally flow from what we do every day, based on the ups and downs of life in community with believers and unbelievers.

READ 1 Peter 3:13–18

LEADER'S NOTE: If our behavior is in alignment with our message, our integrity will eventually be one of the things that attracts the interests of others. If we present the gospel gently and graciously, we avoid being a stumbling block to others. The power of the gospel lies not in our persuasion but in the reality of the gospel itself.

ASK How does Peter link the "reason for the hope that is in you" to the way the gospel changes us?

ASK What attitudes and actions does Peter say we should have as we "give a reason for the hope" that we have? Think about who initiates the conversation here.

LEADER'S NOTE: In the model Peter presents, our actions help initiate conversation. Especially in the workplace, the inquirer should be attracted to the different way we carry ourselves and the different perspective from those around us. Hopefully we seem at odds with the ways of the world in our outlook, gentleness, and respect.

ASK Why is it hard to accept being slandered and treated unfairly "for the reason" we give? Why does Peter say, "Have no fear of them"?

LEADER'S NOTE: Being demeaned or rejected by others is difficult, especially if we believe that our standing in man's eyes is more important than glorifying God. We may make mistakes in how and when we present the gospel, but ultimately it is the gospel that people will accept or reject if we get out of the way and let God speak through us. If we present our hope in Christ, others can ask deeper questions and respond to what God is doing in their lives. We don't have to push them to become converts.

ASK Why is it "better to suffer for doing good . . . than for doing evil"?

LEADER'S NOTE: The prior three questions revolve around the idea that God sees and knows our circumstances. We are to let him judge those who treat us with evil intent and trust that he oversees all of life. Just as Jesus suffered evil and took the sins of his enemies upon himself, we trust that he can do the same thing with our enemies, so that we can return good for evil.

The next passage shows how sharing our faith is a Spirit-empowered process of sowing, watering, growing, and harvesting the gospel. As its messengers God calls us to work in parallel with his Spirit. Because of this we need to be ready to share how the good news is good for us each day.

READ 1 Corinthians 3:6–11

LEADER'S NOTE: The main thrust of this passage is that every part of our work, including the results, are all from God. The purpose in all we do should be to bring glory to God. If we remember that it is God who gives us opportunities to share our faith and he is responsible for the results, we are freed up to be faithful to the opportunities he gives us, whatever they may be.

`ASK` What does Paul mean by "he who plants and he who waters are one"?

`ASK` How does God give the growth in verses 6 and 7?

`ASK` How is Jesus always the foundation of our work? How is this especially true when sharing the message of hope we have?

`TRANSITION TO ARTICLE:` Evangelism has gotten a bad rap, in part because it has often been carelessly and insensitively done. Part of the problem is a one-size-fits-all approach to witnessing that is awkward for everybody; you and everyone else want to avoid it for good reason. But evangelism didn't always have this problem or reputation. Before mass market approaches were applied to everything, including religion, we looked at evangelism and discipleship individually and relationally. If you end up treating people like projects or trophies, they will see through your efforts and either reject you or call you to love more authentically.

How can we learn from the past and move toward a different future in the way we communicate the gospel? We need to think of ways to welcome others authentically, to relate to people personally, and to explain God's big story creatively. Hopefully, *A New Outlook on Neighbors* can help you move beyond fear and shame to find joy and freedom in relating to unbelievers. It's possible if we allow God to help us embody the welcome and peace that flow from the gospel.

ARTICLE *10 minutes*

`TURN TO` *A New Outlook on Neighbors* and read it aloud, taking turns at paragraph breaks.

DISCUSSION *15-20 minutes*

`ASK` What failures have you experienced—on the receiving end or giving end—in past attempts to share your faith?

`ASK` Why might an approach that emphasizes, "Except for the hope of the gospel, we are not much different from those without Christ," be effective?

`ASK` Can you tell a personal story about your relationship with Jesus and the value of that relationship today?

`ASK` Is there someone God is asking you to pursue relationally this week?

EXERCISE *15–25 minutes*

Use the exercise *A Lifestyle of Love* to consider your relationships and how you might sow, water, or harvest in partnership with God's work.

`TURN TO:` *A Lifestyle of Love.* Review with the group if there is time, or assign for homework.

WRAP-UP *5–10 minutes*

Take questions, comments, and lead group in prayer.

LEADER'S GUIDE

EVERYDAY SABBATH:
RESTING FOR WORK *AND* LEISURE

BIG IDEA

Work and leisure are good gifts from God, but they can become idols that pull us from him. In this lesson, we'll look at how a gospel-centered pursuit of rest brings work and leisure back under the authority of God. If we aren't regularly setting aside time for God and his people, our free time can be eaten up in purposeless entertainment and recreation, where we amuse ourselves in self-indulgence. The gospel turns us from self-centered uses of both work and leisure to embrace a genuine *Sabbath* rest.

LESSON OVERVIEW

I. Bible Conversation   Read and talk about the passage(s) [10–20 min]

II. Article   ***Spiritual Rest: How the Gospel Helps Us Unplug*** [10 min]

III. Discussion   Process ***Spiritual Rest: How the Gospel Helps Us Unplug*** article [15–20 min]

IV. Exercise   ***Bringing Sabbath Rest into Every Day of the Week*** [15–25 min]

V. Wrap-Up   Final thoughts and prayer [5–10 min]

BIBLE CONVERSATION *10-20 minutes*

There are two main ways we fail to embrace Sabbath rest. First, we allow everyday preoccupations with work and leisure to crowd out our relationship with God and times of celebration with his people. Regular practices like repenting and trusting daily and pursuing Sabbath rest are used by the Spirit to reorient our lives around our need for God and his love for us. Otherwise we may live unexamined, boundary-less lives and find ourselves working endlessly for goals that other forces dictate. Or, if we *are* able to slow down, the overwhelming pressures of school, home, or workplace can drive us emotionally toward fear and spiritual distraction. Second, just as we often separate spirituality from our workweek, we can also see weekends and holidays merely as times for hobbies, sports, and entertainment. We can be consumed with play, pursuing a rest that always feels just out of reach, instead of enjoying each day in the presence and worship of God. Our society defines leisure negatively as time spent away from work. But without God, it is a counterfeit rest that can breed dissatisfaction and restlessness.

In the workplace the weekend can be synonymous with "on your own time," which implies that you are owned and controlled by others the rest of the time. And because technology allows us to be continually connected, many never truly vacate their callings, even for leisure. We schedule vacations and travel so tightly that many return to work exhausted, ready for the rest and refreshment of a predictable schedule. Our time is all mixed in and all mixed up.

SET-UP Leisure, like work, is not a bad thing, but unmoored from faith, it can fill us with unrest. Leisure apart from God and his people might be a diversion from work, but it cannot provide any spiritually valuable effect. We don't need a work ethic as much as we need a better Sabbath rest ethic.

A gospel-centered approach to Sabbath rest reorders and redefines both work and leisure. It is built upon the coming reality of Jesus's future Sabbath rest, when all creation will be made new to live a life with God in his reordered kingdom. The gospel helps us approach Sabbath rest in ways not possible in the pursuit of work or leisure alone. It reminds us of who God is and who he has made us to be so that we can embrace his purposes in all we do rather than pursue personal schemes and selfish idolatries.

The two passages we'll consider reveal what a huge gift God gave a fallen humanity in the practice of a one-in-seven-day Sabbath. First we'll look to some of the finer details of God resting on the seventh day of creation (Genesis 2:1–3). Then we'll look to the New Testament and some of the ways that Jesus completes and fulfills the Sabbath rest of creation.

READ Genesis 2:1–3

ASK What do you think it means that God's work was finished on the seventh day?

LEADERS NOTE: God's work of creation was full, or fulfilled, on that day. There was more providential and redemptive work to come. But as Genesis 2:3 says, the work of creation was complete and worthy of God setting it apart and making it holy by his rest.

ASK What does it mean that God would rest from work? Does he stop being God?

What is he doing here and why?

ASK How do you think God's work "in creation" was made holy by his rest?

ASK Exodus 20:8–11 points back to this moment in Genesis 2 and tells Israel to imitate God in his pattern of rest. How might imitating God in his rest help us?

LEADERS NOTE: Somehow God's rest is actually sanctifying or setting apart the creation, and his rest represents the real fulfillment or completion of the "worth" of the work itself. Somehow for us as re-creators there is value in giving work the weight and value it deserves by reflecting on it in Sabbath rest. All this is done and empowered by God's underlying activity that undergirds what we do to make it happen and our particular giftedness to re-create or transform his work in light of creation, providence, and redemption.

ARTICLE *10 minutes*

`TURN TO` the article *Spiritual Rest: How the Gospel Helps Us Unplug* and read it aloud, taking turns at paragraph breaks.

DISCUSSION *15–20 minutes*

`ASK` Can you relate to any of the activities mentioned at the beginning of the article (i.e., being constantly plugged in, constantly busy, never resting)? Which bullet point best describes your life?

`ASK` What do you need rest from? How do you think coming to Jesus in faith and repentance might bring rest from what you are working toward?

`ASK` What are some ways you might live out Sabbath rest every day?

`ASK` Have you ever thought about taking one day of the week to rest in order to focus on your relationship with God? What would be hard about that? What might be good about it?

EXERCISE *15–25 minutes*

We've been thinking about Sabbath rest. Use the exercise *Bringing Sabbath Rest into Every Day of the Week* to help you assess how you view the Sabbath and how you might view it differently.

`TURN TO:` *Bringing Sabbath Rest into Every Day of the Week.* Review with the group if there is time or assign for homework.

WRAP-UP *5–10 minutes*

Take questions, comments, and lead group in prayer.

Now let's look at Hebrews 4 where we see a glimpse of Jesus's future work and rest.

READ Hebrews 4:8–16

ASK What do you think it means when it says that there is another day of rest coming "later on" and that the way to enter this future rest is to rest from our works, just as God did?

ASK How does this passage say that we should enter this coming rest

---

LEADERS NOTE: The passage says ironically that (1) we should strive to rest, and (2) we should hold fast to our confession. This second image should conjure up the picture of Israel holding fast to God as their only hope that we saw back in Lesson 5. Jesus's life, death, and resurrection is our only hope for real rest. He achieves for us what we canno achieve for ourselves. He has perfectly obeyed the law, taken our sin upon himself, and given us his righteous record. What we need to mov toward is a deep rest in him, instead of running from him. Our wo is one of repentance where we let him lift off our sin and put on us h righteous record rather than foolishly clinging to our own record. F burden is easy and his yoke is light. If we let him do the work, we w find that his work is no work for us at all, only joy.

ASK How does this rest of Jesus parallel God's rest in Genesis 2?

LEADERS NOTE: God/Jesus goes before us in it. Jesus is sanctif and completing his work (us) by entering into his rest and takir rightful place as Messiah and king.

ASK What are some implications of this kind of rest for us?

TRANSITION TO ARTICLE: We are now going to think more a ways that rest, work, and leisure interact with each other by rea discussing *Spiritual Rest: How the Gospel Helps Us Unplug.*

Now let's look at Hebrews 4 where we see a glimpse of Jesus's future work and rest.

`READ` Hebrews 4:8–16

`ASK` What do you think it means when it says that there is another day of rest coming "later on" and that the way to enter this future rest is to rest from our works, just as God did?

`ASK` How does this passage say that we should enter this coming rest?

LEADERS NOTE: The passage says ironically that (1) we should strive to rest, and (2) we should hold fast to our confession. This second image should conjure up the picture of Israel holding fast to God as their only hope that we saw back in Lesson 5. Jesus's life, death, and resurrection is our only hope for real rest. He achieves for us what we cannot achieve for ourselves. He has perfectly obeyed the law, taken our sins upon himself, and given us his righteous record. What we need to move toward is a deep rest in him, instead of running from him. Our work is one of repentance where we let him lift off our sin and put on us his righteous record rather than foolishly clinging to our own record. His burden is easy and his yoke is light. If we let him do the work, we will find that his work is no work for us at all, only joy.

`ASK` How does this rest of Jesus parallel God's rest in Genesis 2?

LEADERS NOTE: God/Jesus goes before us in it. Jesus is sanctifying and completing his work (us) by entering into his rest and taking his rightful place as Messiah and king.

`ASK` What are some implications of this kind of rest for us?

`TRANSITION TO ARTICLE:` We are now going to think more about the ways that rest, work, and leisure interact with each other by reading and discussing *Spiritual Rest: How the Gospel Helps Us Unplug.*

ARTICLE *10 minutes*

`TURN TO` the article ***Spiritual Rest: How the Gospel Helps Us Unplug***
and read it aloud, taking turns at paragraph breaks.

DISCUSSION *15-20 minutes*

`ASK` Can you relate to any of the activities mentioned at the beginning
of the article (i.e., being constantly plugged in, constantly busy, never
resting)? Which bullet point best describes your life?

`ASK` What do you need rest from? How do you think coming to Jesus in
faith and repentance might bring rest from what you are working toward?

`ASK` What are some ways you might live out Sabbath rest every day?

`ASK` Have you ever thought about taking one day of the week to rest
in order to focus on your relationship with God? What would be hard
about that? What might be good about it?

EXERCISE *15-25 minutes*

We've been thinking about Sabbath rest. Use the exercise ***Bringing
Sabbath Rest into Every Day of the Week*** to help you assess how you
view the Sabbath and how you might view it differently.

`TURN TO:` ***Bringing Sabbath Rest into Every Day of the Week.*** Review
with the group if there is time or assign for homework.

WRAP-UP *5-10 minutes*

Take questions, comments, and lead group in prayer.